TTER

BEYOND W.O.W.®!

Best Wishes!
Jeff

Enjoy!
Dave S.

BEYOND W.O.W.®!

Building Essential
Service-Leadership©
Approaches to Exceptional
Customer Service
Performance & Relationships!

Business/Leadership/Management/Self Help

Library of Congress
Cataloging-in-Publication Data

Magee, Jeffrey L. Ph.D., PDM, CSP, CMC
Golden, Myra MHR
BEYOND WOW©! Building Essential Service-Leadership© Approaches to Exceptional Customer Service Performance & Relationships!

Hannesson, Robb, Project Manager
Jackson-Wolf, Kathy, Copy Editor
King, Stephen, Book Cover Design
Shoemaker, John, Photographer

For information regarding special discounts for bulk purchases for business training emersion, large groups, families and gifts, please contact the following:

Published By: ***PERFORMANCE® Publications***
P.O. Box 701918
Tulsa, OK 74170-1918
Toll free 1-877-90-MAGEE or
918-499-8870

ISBN: 0-9718010-3-7

BEYOND W.O.W.®!

Building Essential Service-Leadership© Approaches to Exceptional Customer Service Performance & Relationships!

By: Myra Golden, MHR
Dr. Jeffrey Magee, PDM/CSP/CMC

Beyond WOW!
ISBN: 0-9718010-3-7
US $29.95

Table of Contents

Foreward

Lots of reading materials cross my desk and/or flash upon my desktop's screen each day. I must admit I take maximum advantage of too few of them. But recently I found myself impressed with the quality, the practicality, the reasonableness and the honesty of words shared by one Dr. Jeff Magee. I'm not sure exactly how I ended up as a recipient of his newsletters and columns, but I knew I liked what I was reading and I looked forward to receiving the benefit of his advice and counsel. Although his focus was "business," much of what he was talking about had direct and current implication for the issues with which Tulsa Public Schools deals day in and day out. I found myself making copies of most of his stuff for continuing reference in my own deliberations concerning the future of TPS.

Shortly thereafter I, quite by happenstance, heard Dr. Magee being interviewed on a local Tulsa radio station. He was asked about his work with companies and corporations around the world and after he detailed some of his experiences, the interviewer wondered aloud why Tulsa organizations did not take better advantage of his talents and abilities since he called Tulsa his home. I resolved then and there to contact his offices and to begin to explore the potential he and his company had for assisting us in striving to be the very best we can be. And the rest is history!

After a few conversations with a Jeff Magee International, Inc. staff member and Dr. Magee himself, and a more thorough look at published materials and accomplishments,

I resolved to attempt to incorporate his expertise into my plans relative to improving our opportunities to better serve our schools, parents and students. I was convinced that his advice about marketing, customer service, leadership, personal/professional development and organizational performance were right on target with our needs and aspirations as a public education enterprise. If I could only figure out a way to secure and sustain his services over an extended timeframe long enough to assure that we could reap maximum benefit I would be very pleased. I was not interested in just a "dose" of his tonic followed by hope for lasting effect and then business as usual. I wanted our team to have him as a resource over time.

Fortunately for TPS we have been able to strike a wonderful deal with the company for a full year of Dr. Magee's time and attention. Included in the deal is participation of the members of TPS' Leadership Team in several of Dr. Magee's ongoing programs and activities and a monthly visit by him, in person, to our team meetings. This copy of Beyond WOW *for each member of our team is also a part of the deal. I commend it to you and invite you to join me as we take a special journey together over the course of the coming year with Dr. Jeff Magee as our guide!*

Best wishes.

Dave Sawyer
Superintendent,
Tulsa Public Schools

Preface

Finding W.O.W.® and Why "Service-Leadership©" Lead Customer Service Is Hard To Find…

So there we were. We entered the Doubletree Hotel (a nationally known chain hotel) for lunch at one of their WOW® restaurants, and while living in the neighborhood we did not meet the traditional client profile for a hotel restaurant. So why would we patronize this as our eating option of choice?

Maybe it has something to do with the WOW® factor delivered by Jimmy Sanders the Manager (his assistant Elba or their predecessor Alex or Kal and their legacies left) or any one of the explosive lead servers such as Felicia McGee, Hamed, Susan, Judy, Mary, Huda, or Mo. Or maybe even in the personal ownership and attention to detail by Kerry or any of the other restaurant support staff.

Not only do they all make every customer feel welcomed and greet you by name (they consistently ask for it if they don't recognize you; and that indicates that they have discovered how to attract non traditional customers to their business), they ensure your every need is always taken care of, they routinely gush in appreciation for your patronage, and they routinely back this up with meaningful gestures – that is WOW®!

Unfortunately, this has become a rare experience by the customer.

It would seem that business has entered a new era of competing to see how bad the actual service can be and still maintain a customer base. Have you ever noticed this, at the precise moment you hand over your hard-earned money to a merchant, and wonder just how they stay in business?

It would seem that the era of poor customer service has become sport. In fact, you might even wonder if there are special training camps for these service providers to attend that demonstrate heightened levels of "crappy customer service, actions, behavior and attitude!"

Low service and even no service is the new norm and to expect service with a smile is a lesson most only read about in history books…

It would leave one wondering aloud if there were some sort of Olympics for "Crappy Customer Service" that businesses and individuals compete to beat out the last experience of leadership—less customer service exchanges.

We have evolved into such a state of poor service for what is supposed to be a service economy that many people cry out not for any level of awesome or W.O.W.® service, but just a fair, honorable, ethical, integrity-based service experience.

This begs the question, "Where have all of the Service-Leadership© professionals gone and why doesn't anyone take responsibility to grow and model positive behaviors and attitudes that can in actuality allow anyone to attain W.O.W.®?"

Further compounding the impact of building a profitable relationship with the customer is the realization that customer service creates "experiences" and it is the Service-Leadership© approach that leads every person to recognize what "acts" lead to a positive service "experience." It is these individual "experiences" that manifests into positive attitudes and constructive W.O.W.® "experiences!"

The examples of businesses that make a profit in trying times and within industries where others around them are either filing for bankruptcy or struggling to survive do exist. A culture of entitlement, over paid employees (at every level of an organization) and even in some cases managers and unions that encourage substandard performance from those around them, all add to a climate of combative customer service exchanges.

To earn the experience of W.O.W.® in a customer's mind today, alarmingly, does not really take very much effort. In fact, if one actually calculated the specific acts that rate as a W.O.W.® experience, these should, in fact, be the norm of business transactions experienced across the scale of customer transactions.

WOW *would be any act that rises to the level of* ***"Wonderfully Obvious What's"*** *... those "what factors" that compel others to want that same experience or item – what others want as well!*

The answer to why this does not occur more often comes down to a lack of Service-Leadership© ability on the part of those at the top line and frontline management alike!

In this publication you will learn the tactical and strategic measures necessary to attain a W.O.W.® level of service in every interaction with a customer (internally or externally). And, how to confidently assume a Service-Leader mentality to ensure increased market share and market loyalty in what others see as a difficult market today!

This publication will detail the steps to sustained W.O.W.® Service-Leadership© by all players in a business at every level and at every opportunity. You will learn how to move beyond just growth and to significant levels of profitability. So the next time you believe the customer service representative before you would rather you "SHUT UP, Because No One Cares," ask yourself if you or your organization might be doing similar acts with your customers.

So the obvious objective that this text will address for you, and those within your business, is the W.O.W.® factors, the

"Wonderfully Obvious What's" …

1. ***What can I do to strive as a Service-Leader to provide as a minimum course of action every time?***

2. ***How easy can I establish a lasting relationship with the customer by moving beyond that act?***

The Service-Leader approach recognizes that the customer contact opportunity is the greatest opportunity to generate revenue and save revenue for an organization, which ensures a healthy organization.

The Service-Leader understands that there are two ways to grow a business, and only two. Every strategy and every tactical activity must address these for both survival and growth of an organization. Far too often, what organizations do is to stifle future success by focusing on short term actions that address only one of these points.

1. A business must continually address how to generate the circulation of monies internally to their market (this would be the connection of present customers and the associated business transactions with them); and

2. A business must then address the circulation from external sources (the cultivation of new business relationships) that would otherwise never enter their market.

A good example of this dilemma would be a municipality or state government, not understanding this, would focus solely on how to connect or stimulate the economy within its borders and does nothing to attract or reward those people that bring money into it from elsewhere. What it is doing is limiting its customer contact service and growth actions and this is typically done from either a lack of knowledge or outright scarcity (fear) mentality.

This book will illustrate how to address both the internal and external forces simultaneously for success … getting Beyond W.O.W.® for a lasting legacy of greatness!

PART ONE – Building A Stable Foundation:

Chapter One—
The Baseline of Successful Customer Service

Chapter Two—
The Shift in Business DNA: To Attain W.O.W.® Standing with Customers, 5-MAPs are Necessary

Chapter Three—
Measuring What One Cares About: Customers Want Only Four Things

Chapter Four—
Quality Care … Ways to Fast Track What You Do and What Must be Provided to the Customer for W.O.W.®

Chapter One - *The Baseline of Successful Customer Service…*

Service-Leadership©, at the most basic level and with each person, starts with an incredibly expense-free variable. Yet, it is amazing how many organizations miss the true secret to customer service success and the ability to deliver W.O.W.® While it seems to evade most individuals placed into engaging customers, it is top of mind for every individual who encounters customer service care providers.

WOW *would be any act that rises to the level of* ***"Wonderfully Obvious What's"*** *… (as detailed in the PREFACE) those "what factors" that compel others to want that same experience or item – what others want as well!*

While this secret ingredient is unpopular in adult circles of conversation, it can't be refuted.

To deliver W.O.W.® to your customer and to bring out the best in one's Service-Leadership© ability, start with what Professor William James more than one-hundred years ago found to be the foundation to his studies within human psychology. B.F. Skinner and Dr. Albert Ellis also concluded this factor to be the single most common denominator among all humans. It is this factor that we all have one-hundred percent (100%) control over and that influences our actions and reactions.

Have you guessed that secret variable yet? If not, the answer is "ATTITUDE."

Then so too, the foundation to Service-Leadership© effectiveness and success is within one's ATTITUDE. How one draws upon this variable constructively to influence both actions (logic based behaviors) and reactions (emotional based behaviors) is one's baseline to successful customer success!

Here's a better secret. Don't hire people with combative, arrogant, ego-driven attitudes and place them in positions of direct contact with those that bring money (your life blood!) to you!

Create an environment conducive for winning attitudes to shine and watch your service level shine. If the service level is down, look in the mirror and check your attitude. They are typically inter-connected.

To identify "how" and "what" one's attitude telegraphs to others, consider:

1. The tone of voice.

2. Body language.

3. Dress, wardrobe and its appearance.

4. Attentiveness to those that can bring future business and influence others.

5. The level of energy one has on a regular basis over the areas of responsibility.

6. One's willingness to assist in positions that connect immediately before and after theirs in a line of functionality.

As a Service-Leader, the way you view and treat customers has a profound effect on how your employees will view and treat customers. Do you speak positively about customers? What about the demanding, unreasonable, or irate customers? The Service-Leader must be a role model of good service in ALL situations and interactions, including interactions with internal customers.

The "Service-Leader" demonstrates W.O.W.® internal customer service with peers, employees, bosses, and in department-to-department relations by being positive, responsive, willing, and eager. If you don't treat your colleagues and employees to W.O.W.® service, how will you instill a W.O.W.® attitude to the frontline?

The Service-Leader realizes that ATTITUDE is actually 100% of the game all of the time. Psychology shows that one's mindset/attitude directly influences one's actions. The Service-Leader rises to any occasion to deliver WOW to the end user or beneficiary of what they do.

If you strive to deliver 100% of your ability 100% of the time, here is a simple alphanumeric game:

Take each letter of the alphabet, from letter "A to Z," and associate a number value to each letter, starting with number one for "A" and number two for letter "B" onward. Then, recognize that the corresponding number value for each letter in the word "ATTITUDE" added together equals _____ percent?

The baseline for W.O.W.® customer service starts with attitude. Before skill, ability, training initiatives, rewards systems and engagement opportunities, it starts with whether an individual has the proper attitude and thus, the desire to engage others as a Service-Leader. If individuals and organizations fail to act accordingly, then extinction may become their reality.

Are you an expense or revenue generator in your interactions with others?

The bottom line to business success is whether a member of the team is a revenue generator or an expense. Service-Leadership© is one's ability to demonstrate that they are revenue generators to their business!

Another aspect of the attitudinal influence on positive customer service relationships and influencing lasting relationships, sits upon the realization that every interaction with a customer, good or bad, furthers that customer's "experience" with you. Their walk away "experiences" impact how they see you, respond to and engage you. To determine how best to engage others view attitude as a teeter-totter with a level plank upon it. Every positive and negative "experience" is placed atop the plank, one side for positive and the other side negative. As you engage your customers, knowing how their plank leans will indicate what actions are necessary to attain positive customer interactions. Conversely, if a customer has a negative or combative attitude, then the specific acts necessary to neutralize that attitude and then influence it in a positive direction become clear.

Your attitude and their attitude combine for the Service-Leader W.O.W.® factor!

Have you ever left a customer service interaction where the service provider had such a sincere, appreciative, positive attitude in your presence, that you actually heard yourself talking to yourself about how soon you could get back there for another serving of that experience?

Attitude makes an organization and attitude becomes the magnet by which people are compelled to come back again and again!

Chapter Two - *The Shift in Business DNA: To Attain W.O.W.® Standing With Customers, 5-MAPs are Necessary*

Maximizing customer contact and determining how to attain or maintain a W.O.W.® status, starts with the make-up of leadership personalities, advocate expectations, influence centers, expectations and desires, and the over-all commitment of front line contacts. All of this is what is referred to as the DNA of the business.

Expectations, reputations, commitment, role accountabilities and the infrastructure in place to create and reinforce professionalism at the highest level all add to what a business' DNA is and will be. If W.O.W.® is desired, yet reality is that the leadership team and customer contact individuals (inclusive of any traditional management and labor union behaviors) scream out that one actually seeks opportunities to provide minimal effort for expected maximum reward, then W.O.W.® will remain allusive!

To create a DNA for success, ask yourself these questions and reflect upon ways to attain each or "Plus-It©" (meaning to take anything that you already are known for as W.O.W.® and explore ways to improve it just one degree – Plus-It), if you feel you are already there. Consider:

1. What do I do to champion and celebrate individual successes on the team?

2. What do I do to acknowledge and celebrate repeat business?

3. What do I do to communicate lessons learned when overcoming a challenge?

4. What do I do on a regular basis to celebrate the opportunities available and bring about fun to the position?

5. What do we or I do when the customer is not present to foster a healthy relationship among us?

To attain the highest level of customer contact, consider how your customers view you and how they score your service level.

There are two ways a customer can score the interactions with business today. They either receive something from you that they measure:

1. Physically; or
2. Emotionally

There are two sides to every customer interaction transaction. These two sides of W.O.W.® are the front-side and backside as perceived by the customer. The front-side is measured in the form of the tangible (physical factor) that the customer seeks or receives or in essence, the "What factor." And the backside is measured in the form of the emotional or psychological or the "How factor" of how the other perceives you.

Physical deliverables and missed deliverables are easy to address. The shipment did not arrive in time. This is a physical, it is easy to see and measure. One's mind can be triggered into exploring a host of ways to address this, correct this, right this with the customer and ensure it does not happen again. And, with the strategic deployment of action, you can convert this negative Physical into a neutral and then onward to a positive experience for the customer.

However, with an Emotional (psychological) customer, the experience resonates with the customer for an extended period of time, and this can be both more challenging to get the customer to reveal to you and require a longer commitment to converting from a negative to a positive. If a customer orders a meal and halfway through their meal they look down and see a bug climbing out from under their food, there will be a lasting, horrific, "emotional" impression in their mind of that experience. This becomes a true test of your Service-Leadership© abilities!

Likewise, a positive emotional experience that a customer has with you goes a long way in gaining leverage when a potential problem does arise.

Again, to make the shift within an organization's DNA to ensure every customer interaction, at every level and by every point-of-contact is a W.O.W.® experience, view all that you do on two levels:

1. Physical; or
2. Emotional

You will know if you and your organization have the basic DNA make-up to attain this or maintain a positive environment, based upon how every person at every level within an organization demonstrates their Service-Leadership© behaviors when engaging the end user customer.

To ensure peak performance by every member of an organization and to ensure that decisions being made are congruent with the health of the over-all organization's DNA, consider the level of clarity that every member of the present team has with that organization's Mission Statements.

If you will consider that tradition has it that a high priced consultant, typically one that has never signed a paycheck, is brought in to work with senior leaders to craft an organization's Mission Statement. Then, that mission statement is proudly placed on the wall with great fanfare and reverence. The following day, everyone continues on their way daily, with little or no regard for what the mission statement conveys. Realizing this, then one can grasp an easier understanding as to why most front line customer service professionals have no idea what they say, much less what they are supposed to be conveying in relationship to an organization's attempt at reaching W.O.W.®!

So what is needed in crafting effective Service-Leadership© DNA and ensuring that it remains healthy into the future?

A set of MAPs© (Mental Action Plans, by which to guide one's actions, as first presented in ***YIELD MANAGEMENT: The Leadership Alternative To Performance and Net Profit Improvement***, by CRC Press/St. Lucie Press. ISBN# 1-57444-206-6 / USA $39.95, www.JeffreyMagee.com/library.asp) will aid in attaining W.O.W.® and these MAPs© are what many in the business context would call Mission Statements.

To enhance the Service-Leadership© effectiveness of present customer service stars and enable others to aspire to the level of greatness that lies within them, consider how best to craft the following sequential descending "Five Service-Leadership© Mission Statements:"

1. ***Organizational***—The core stakeholders to an organization that have vested financial interest and serve as the senior leadership team are charged with crafting this mission statement. It should address the Who, What, When, Where, Why, and How aspects of that organization when completed.

2. ***Functional Business Unit***—Each work area to an organization should also have a mission statement, following the same formula as detailed above. By examining the over-all organization's Mission Statement, Service-Leaders stars recognize that each business unit merely contributes to that over-all statement and, once defined, guides all decisions.

   Everyone within that business unit should actively participate in crafting this one, and each should sign it before it is posted as a daily beacon to guide all of our customer interactions!

3. ***Customer***—This can be a moving, fluid target for many service providers. So, the key is to be able to recognize independent of previous engagements, when face-to-face with a customer, "What is their purpose, need, want, mission statement and how do I fulfill that?"

4. ***Colleague***—To recognize the core motivational reasons why the colleague you

interact with is employed, reveals to you how to engage them to encourage their participation in providing W.O.W.® level Service-Leadership© to customers!

5. ***Self***—With the insight gained from evaluating the first four core organizational influencing Mission Statements, you can now craft the map that will guide you to your goals as well.

   With the gained perspective of these five, you are more likely to provide to all five W.O.W.® levels of service.

The shift in business DNA to attain and sustain business W.O.W.® can be subtle or dramatic. In either case, customer service providers, whether they be at the front-line, bottom-line or top-line, must all have a universal MAP if they are to compliment one another's abilities and energies for a lasting W.O.W.® legacy!

Benchmark your actions against these five Mission Statements. Ask yourself if you have these clearly defined and whether they are posted at the present time. If so, write down your perception of each and then engage all of your colleagues or employees and determine if your perception is consistent with each other.

When organizations allow good people to work interactively with customers and have not clearly gained consensus from all employees as to what that Mission Statement, in fact, is good people begin to work against one another and place customers into positions of confrontation with fellow employees over what is acceptable and unacceptable customer service behaviors and expectations!

Only when everyone is playing from the same Mission Statement perspective (game plan) can an entire team build off of one another, compliment one another and attain success with one another!

Once this is attained, then an environment (DNA) can be structured and reinforced that empowers every customer contact professional with the authority within their area to address any customer, at any time, on any issue and make an informed, profit-based business oriented command decision.

And with this DNA, product extensions and innovations will occur.

Chapter Three -
Measuring What One Cares About: Customers Want Only Four Things

The adage of what gets measured gets attention is true in the business of attaining W.O.W.®

One of the leading non-governmental or patrician entities in the United States tracking customer service data of the past generation is a group called, The FORUM Group. They reinforce the reasons we have found as to why customers leave, why customers would be compelled to look for another place to take their business and where each person within an organization has an ability to excel in their Service-Leadership© ability.

Through the FORUM Group, it has been determined that customers leave for four primary reasons:

1. Financial—They believe there is either a more fiscal option that they are being overcharged and under delivered, or budget issues, unjustified rising price points, etc…

2. Needs—They believe that what they need is not offered or is no longer offered by their present supplier or partnership…

3. Perception—The customer arrives at a belief that they are no longer appreciated or valued by the service provider, and that the service provider finds them, as the customer, to be an inconvenience…

4. Communication—There is a problem that develops out of miss communication, poor communication, negative communication, too much communication or just no communication that leads the customer to believe they are not appreciated.

The power of this revelation is that for every Service-Leader provider, the latter two can be personally addressed and corrected. The last two are within everyone's control to do something about (review Chapter Twenty-Two for dozens of action oriented ways to do this), if they truly believe that what they have to offer or provide is W.O.W.®!

The first two are within grasp, control and change by the senior members of an organization. If there is a DNA climate that allows frontline providers to provide these findings when they arise to the senior leaders, then they can determine when and how to address these to attain W.O.W.®!

"On any given day, senior management can accurately identify about three to seven percent of operational problems. Mid level management can accurately identify about fourteen percent, and the frontline customer contact professional can accurately identify about forty-four percent accurately.

Within traditionally structured business, you can see that no one person really has a pulse on what is happening. Combined, all still cannot see 100% of the picture accurately. It is paramount for all to collaboratively work together to ensure customer success and effectiveness," according to the Wharton School of Business.

What gets measured gets addressed. To build greater productivity and profitability within your business, identify what needs to be measured.

While effective Service-Leadership© demands detailed survey management (*survey systems will be addressed in later chapters*), immediate feedback should be consistently and repeatedly gathered based upon these questions:

1. Do you provide a service or product?

2. Do you primarily engage external or internal customers?

3. What piece of the Five Service-Leadership© Mission Statements is your primary responsibility?

Your ability to recognize this need will be the catalyst in recognizing how to immediately measure oneself in the presence of a customer and how to hold oneself accountable for Service-Leadership© excellence!

Based upon what you provide and your level of participation in delivering this to the customer, determine corrective engagement action plans for that customer who comes to you for any one of the above four exit reasons.

Chapter Four -

Quality Care…
Ways to Fast Track What You Do and What Must be Provided to the Customer for W.O.W.®

A way to measure what one delivers to a customer at the most fundamental level for immediate success can be measured with the **RELIABLE C.A.R.E.©** formula.

For several years and across three continents, while conducting Service-Leadership© focused executive development programs, *JEFF MAGEE INTERNATIONAL/JMI, Inc.* surveyed and collected information from more than 10,000 participants on customer service issues. Surveyed questions, "When you are the customer and spend your hard-earned money, what do you look for from the vendor you go to? Conversely, if they did not provide you "X," you would look for another vendor-partner?"

The responses were powerful and consistent across the board and from every section of organizational structures. The responses fell into five distinctive categories. A customer wants to do business with another person or organization that is:

4. **Reliable (R)**—Do you do what you say? Do you deliver what you purport to be able to deliver. Do those associated with you live up to the standards you have set before them?

5. **Care (C)**—Do you demonstrate that you "appreciate" the customer? And, how do you communicate that to the customer – in gesture or words? How often?

6. **Attractive (A)**—Are you an appealing option and do you yell out that you elevate the customer standing in life by them connecting with you? Others measure this by first impressions and by whether you elevate another's reputation or standing in life. What does your physical environment (facility, office, building, lobby, plant, parking lot, driveway, etc.) say about you and how you greet those that come to you?

7. **Responsive(R)**—Do you respect the customer enough to engage them in a timely or expeditious manner? How quickly do you follow up with customers or return calls and email to them? Do you return information and requests quickly or do you delay in rcsponding to such a level that this compounds upset customers?

8. **Empathy (E)**—Do you simply acknowledge the customer? This does not mean you take their side, challenge them, agree nor disagree with them. Simply, do you convey basic dignity and respect towards them?

So, if you can use this **Reliable C.A.R.E.** formula as a benchmark in evaluating your personal engagements with customers and score high marks in each category, then and only then do you arrive at the right to hold your peers accountable to deliver the same.

Consider designing a fast, simple evaluation grid for each of these "letters" and asking your valued customers to occasionally score you. Compare their feedback to how you would have scored yourself. You can use a score template of:

1. 0-2 points = did not meet customer expectations
2. 3 points = met customer expectation
3. 4+ points= exceeded customer expectations

You could further enhance the effectiveness of such a score grid by asking the same questions to RCARE for both the human equation (you) and the product equation (what they received that you delivered or facilitated).

This is a powerful means to influence the DNA of an organization to become W.O.W.® oriented and Service-Leadership© focused!

This formula can be used as a template when interacting with any customer. You can reference any or all of these categories when designing a survey questionnaire to solicit feedback from happy, unknown customers and upset customers to gain their insight as to how they rate you in each category. Their feedback, whether in a phone conversation transaction, face-to-face interaction or other format can be valuable in determining future courses of action and interaction.

This insight can also aid in determining future product or service expansions, determining where to address labor attention and additions to process improvements for the sake of the customer to your core business!

PART TWO – Fast-Tracking Customer Service for Increased Revenue:

Chapter Five –
Understanding Customer Service as a Strategic Profit Center & Positioning Yourself for Success

Chapter Six –
Customer Service Index© (CSI)
Reveals How to Improve

Chapter Seven –
Understanding Your "Service-Leadership©"
Engagement Style for Peak Performance

Chapter Five -
Understanding Customer Service As a Strategic Profit Center & Positioning Yourself for Success

The after-shocks of September 11, 2001 (and the terrorist attacks on the World Trade Center Towers in New York City) have made an unprecedented and unthinkable impact on sales and growth in nearly every industry in the U.S. and in some cases, abroad. Massive layoffs, a free-falling stock market and low consumer confidence have agitated an already fragile and recessed economy.

It is during these times of flux that companies must think smarter and more creatively about how to achieve sales growth, and ultimately, how to survive. One proven opportunity for sales and growth, even during an economic downturn, that is often overlooked is for companies to build and maintain loyal relationships with their customers. Another way to state this is for companies to turn customer service into a bona fide profit center.

A critical profit center to any organization is the customer contact or customer service entry and exit points to that organization and the professionals staffing those points of contact.

Far too often leaders feel compelled to place a disproportionate amount of time, energy and finance into research and development and those areas of finding and getting a new customer, and far too little or no time investing inward to their existing client base.

Studies have been initiated over the past few decades on the costs associated with attracting new clients and the costs involved in maintaining a customer. Further, what it costs to develop a raving fan and advocate to your organization Alarmingly, in nearly every study, it costs less to maintain and grow your business from a pre-existing client than it does to matriculate a new customer and grow that account.

Most organizations fail to realize that profit and growth are primarily driven by customer loyalty.

Most companies view and manage customer service as a cost center. In these companies, setting a profit target and working backward to arrive at the required revenue target to attain sales and growth is the undisputed strategic plan. Growth and profit increases are achieved in these companies by focusing entirely on a customer acquisition strategy.

If one is more serious about finding, getting, keeping and growing a customer, then a higher commission, bonus, incentive or pay might be considered for the person on your team who cultivates more business from existing accounts and clients versus simply new accounts. Consider the depth of each existing account (see Chapter Fourteen) in terms of additional advocates to be cultivated and business opportunities to be harvested.

A growth strategy based on both customer acquisition and customer retention is a smarter, sounder plan. Loyalty-leading companies like Disney, Wal-Mart, and Saturn view and manage customer service as a profit center and they have strategically built a base of loyal customers that come back again and again. These customers spend more and more money, and spread positive word-of-mouth advertising.

"It's only a customer, it doesn't matter."

This mentality, will be the wall that impedes these initiatives and successes, and so to becomes that mindset from which competition springs and your clients evolve towards...

Managing customer service as a profit center means fiercely focusing on both increasing customer satisfaction and customer retention. This focus can lead to net profit increases in two dramatic ways, as illustrated below:

- ✍ Small increases in customer satisfaction can lead to BIG net profit. The Marriott Corporation reports that a 1% increase in customer satisfaction at its hotels is worth more than $50 million in sales. Similarly, IBM has found that a 1% increase in customer satisfaction at just one assembly plant is worth more than $275 million over five years.

- ✍ Generally, increasing customer retention by just 5% can lead to a net profit increase to the bottom line of 25% to 85%. (See chapter 16 for a breakdown of how this profit is generated.)

In order for a department or operation to be considered a profit center, it must be doing one of two things for the company:

1. Making money; or
2. Saving money

Customer service doesn't initially present itself as a revenue generating department or a risk management department. But a well-designed and well-implemented customer service strategy, based on building and maintaining loyal relationships with customers, will turn any customer service operation into a profit center. Customer service will be bringing in revenue and cutting costs. Well-run customer service operations impact the company's bottom line in three key ways:

1. **Reduces acquisitions costs and promotes customer retention.** Well-run customer service operations keep more customers and this saves money because most industry experts agree that it costs four to six times more to win a customer than to keep a customer.

2. **Generates positive word-of-mouth advertising.** Customers who perceive their service experience as "truly outstanding" will tell an average of five people about their encounter. This is important because word-of-mouth advertising is the most persuasive form of advertising. When customers spread positive word-of-mouth advertising for a company, they literally become an extension of the sales force.

3. **Increases the profitability of each customer.** An effective customer service strategy not only helps an organization keep more customers, but creates so much value for customers that loyal customers consistently buy more and more products and services from the company's line. They are willing to pay more for these services. When customer profitability is increased, growth through a customer retention strategy can be exponential.

In order to maximize profit potential, any strategic plan for growth and profit increase needs to be based on both customer acquisition and retention. That is, companies must always look for new customers, while at the same time create a service experience of superior value that helps them keep the customers they have and sell more and more to those customers.

Your Unique Selling Feature/Unique Service Features (USF©) Drives Your Differentiators and Allows You to Position Yourself for Success

Understanding customer service as a strategic profit center is critical for a Service-Leader in a competitive market place. Viewing your present customer, potential customer acquisition extensions off of that point-of-contact within an organization, as well as new accounts, all as profit centers is the natural aim of a "Service-Leader" on a daily basis and with every customer service interaction.

Customer service, as a profit center, can be determined by looking at four broad and general *Unique Selling Features* (USF ONE - the tangibles or what factors of the offer from your organization) or four *Unique Service Features* (USF TWO - the intangibles or how factors of what you offer) as detailed below.

There are four immediate ways to differentiate your organization or offer from others and thus four differing ways to deliver customer service, communicate customer service and increase the deliverables around customer service to a customer:

1. **Better**—Customers are looking for quality and quality improvement or enhancement to what they presently are receiving or need in the marketplace. Organizations even center their advertising and promotion efforts, campaigns and budgets on these same areas.

2. **Faster**—Customers are looking for speed and efficiency to what they presently are receiving or

need in the marketplace. Organizations even center their advertising and promotion efforts, campaigns and budgets on these same areas.

3. **Different**—Customers are looking for uniqueness/differences in what they presently are receiving or need in the marketplace, as a way of differentiating themselves from others. Organizations even center their advertising and promotion efforts, campaigns and budgets on these same areas.

4. **Cheaper**—Customers are looking for cost effectiveness to what they presently are receiving or need in the marketplace. Organizations even center their advertising and promotion efforts, campaigns and budgets on these same areas.

In looking at each of these four areas as they relate internally to your organization and with each functional leader, determine ways to provide greater value to every customer by drawing upon each. You may also find value in determining how many added-value points you have in these four categories that an existing client may not realize. By bringing that to their attention, you may enhance existing relationships and enlarge the business with that existing client.

As you read this Chapter, reflect on a personal experience you have right now where you are the customer/patron to a business that truly understands this concept. Then, ask how you can replicate that in what you do and in what your peers should be doing.

An example that may come to mind for many people is perhaps a favorite restaurant or dining experience. Consider:

> While on a business trip from Kansas City, I happened upon a restaurant in Oklahoma that has been featured in several southern society magazines and even on a PBS special. In an industry with national bankruptcy rates among the highest of any individual business segmentation and employee turnover rates that seem to create revolving doors of employment, this restaurant business is known nationally, and it has an average server and kitchen staff tenure of five years or longer.
>
> Employees drive in for miles to work and customers drive in (some even by helicopter) from across the state to take in the unique experience (Different/Better).
>
> Employees on their ten year anniversary receive diamonds. The force behind this example of understanding the customer as the strategic profit center (and this means both taking care of the employees and the end user patron as a customer) is the matriarch of Molly's Landing (3700 Hwy. 66, Catoosa, Oklahoma), Ms. Linda Powell!
>
> Linda and her sons that lead this force (Russ and Doug) understand by continual feedback, analysis of the market and their customer base, what their Unique Selling Feature is and then remain steadfast to it!

You can increase the profitability of your organization through the in-depth analysis of every existing customer contact area. Then, identify ways to educate all service providers to take the lead in their interactions with customers to ensure that they are receiving maximum appropriate goods/services from you for their needs. This is essential to increased gross and net revenues.

Areas to evaluate for increased customer business matriculation could be:

1. In accounting interactions and contact, correspondence, statement and invoice statement-stuffers, etc.

2. In follow up contact after a customer purchase to ensure they are satisfied and make them aware of other parallel offerings.

3. In onsite consultations and review of existing account business and determining if what they are doing is in alignment with their business needs and organization mission statements.

4. In dialogue with clients and then listening closely for opportunities to meet their existing needs and emerging needs with what you have to offer that can be: Better, Faster, Cheaper or Different for their needs opposed to present being patterns or market offerings.

By evaluating the routine functions of what your business provides and the most consistent percentage of customers you serve, you can then benchmark your present and future actions for sustained profitability. Focusing on what you have first and to ensure you keep it and grow it, is in fact a powerful differentiator for strategic profit security to your business.

Let's place this into monetary perspective. In considering all of these actions as they relate to your goal of exceeding BEYOND W.O.W.® concepts, evaluate the value of your customer and thus the over-all “Lifetime Value” of a customer to your business. Consider the following formula as a way of measuring the “Lifetime Value” of a customer you have:

1. Identify a typical customer you engage by name for this formula and write their name down, ______________________.

2. Now identify (an educated guess will do) a typical business transaction with that customer in terms of related dollar amount, $______________.

3. Now identify the number of typical transactions that you have with this customer each month, __________.

4. Take the dollar amount from question two above and multiply that against number four above, $______________________.

5. Now multiply that financial number by twelve (number of months each year) for a total annual financial transaction each year, $_________.

6. How many years has that customer been with your organization, ______________________.

7. Now multiply the financial answer from number five above by the number in item six above, for the

"Lifetime Value" of a customer to your organization, $____________.

Understanding customer service as a legitimate aspect of the over-all business operational model and treating the customer contact aspect of the business as such, will afford an organization a significant market advantage. The Service-Leader must recognize the gravity of positioning and the financial value of a single customer, if it is to truly appreciate a customer and model success to those they lead.

Chapter Six -
Customer Service Index© Reveals How to Improve

Attaining W.O.W.® many times rests upon one's ability to assess each interaction and impending interactions on the run and determine one's best course of actions as to how best to elevate a customer interaction to the level Service-Leadership© success.

Whether your interactions are on a telephone, through email, correspondence, face-to-face or in a group situation, your ability to objectively assess an interaction can dictate the exact way a customer sees you. This, in turn, indicates how your business will grow or die.

Many businesses deliver what they perceive as a level of customer service that ensures success and profitability. In fact, a business that delivers what it feels is "excellent customer care" may, in fact, be one step from that of a "poor service provider." That could be one day from being out of business!

The ***"Customer Service Index©"*** (CSI©) can be administered physically by measuring two stimulants or mentally by visualizing two stimulants. The instrument application will determine precisely how best to engage a customer by:

1. Instant identification of why a customer is upset.

2. Instant identification of how customers measure—see your offering.

3. Instant identification of how to enrich your customer relationship/partnership.

4. Instant identification of whether the organization is carrying the personnel or whether the personnel are carrying the organization.

5. Instant identification of how to score your level of customer care, as either Poor/Excellent/Exceptional.

6. Objectively assess why "excellent" service is more alarming than "poor" service.

To use the CSI Index, visualize an "L-Grid." In engaging customers on the run, you can replicate this model by glancing at your left hand in the "L-Grid" position.

Identify the vertical axis line with the attribution of "PRODUCT/SERVICE" that you provide and attribute the horizontal axis line with the label, "PEOPLE," for how you are perceived by the customer.

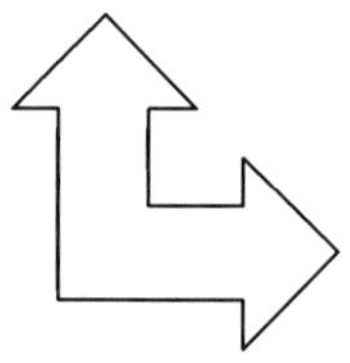

Scoring the axis lines is easy. If you were to score each line from zero at the bottom and ten at the high/outward end of the line, you can then score the half-way-point (a five) as the difference between low and high scores. Low equates poor/low measurements and higher scores equate to excellent/high scores.

Methodology: The lower the score on the vertical and horizontal axis lines, the lower the number.

1. **Bottom Left Quadrant Measurement**—If the customer scores the Service-Leader provider's product/service as low and the level of personalization as low, then that bottom left quadrant of the CSI© would be identified as "POOR SERVICE." Imagine how long you would remain in business if you remained in this quadrant. This implies what you provide is unimpressive and does not meet expectations, while at the same time the delivery system (people) is unimpressive and did not meet expectations.

   Both the people and product aspects need immediate radical attention if you are to remain in business. The sole reason you are in business at this moment is because your customers are being held hostage and have no other available options—for now!

2. **Top Left Quadrant Measurement**—If the customer scores the Service-Leader provider's product/service as high and the level of personalization as low, then that top left quadrant of the CSI would be identified as "EXCELLENT SERVICE." This label should strike you as incorrect, although it is accurate—but very misleading for leaders. Another label for this top left quadrant is 'Brand Loyalty.'

The brand/product/service being offered is carrying the team/personnel. While the customers' expectations with respect to what they are receiving are being met or exceeded, it is the personnel that do not meet or exceed expectations.

When a suitable alternative enters the market, your perceived loyal customers will revolt and leave in mass exodus for the alternative product/service. Immediate attention to the team is called for here.

3. **Bottom Right Quadrant Measurement**—If the customer scores the Service-Leader provider's product/service as low and the level of personalization as high, then this bottom right quadrant of the CSI© would be identified as "EXCELLENT SERVICE." This label should also strike you as incorrect, although it is accurate—however, it is very misleading for leaders. Another label for this bottom right quadrant is 'People Loyalty.'

   The people delivering the product/service are carrying the organization. As the customer's' expectations with respect to what they are receiving is not being met or exceeded. When the person they are loyal to leaves that business, so too will their patronage as they seek out suitable alternatives.

   Immediate attention must be given to improving the product/service and finding a way to attain W.O.W.® with it, as your people are becoming exhausted over compensating for deliverable problems.

4. **Top Right Quadrant Measurement**—If the customer scores the Service-Leader provider's product/service as high and the level of personalization as high, then the top right quadrant of the CSI© would be identified as "EXCEPTIONAL SERVICE."

   This top right quadrant is where a true customer relationship is attained. When there is a problem, it is here that a customer is most inclined to work with you and not see the problem, as a problem.

   It is here that the customer's expectations in both what he or she is receiving in relationship to the product/service and the people are being met and oftentimes exceeded. This relationship is where lasting loyalty develops, and this is where a customer evolves into an advocate for you and champions you to others.

The applications for the CSI are explosive. You can reference this model when confronted by an angry, upset, hostile, discouraged or simply any customer interaction.

By listening to the other person and glancing at your left hand in the "L-Grid" position, you can now listen to their comments and benchmark them against this model. Based upon where their words intersect the two lines, you now know precisely how best to engage them to maintain top right quadrant or to move them toward the top right quadrant.

You can use this model to evaluate your competition through the eyes of their customer to determine competitive advantage points, to determine potential areas for improvement within your business and to recognize possible business growth opportunities.

You can use the model to facilitate survey interviews with your top customers to determine why they come to you as opposed to why you feel they come to you. For example, you may believe you are delivering "Exceptional Service" presently to your top clients, but now you can design a set of questions for both the vertical and horizontal axis lines to evaluate. Then, listen to the responses to determine where your clients place you, as opposed to where you may have felt you occupied.

From a managerial perspective (whether you are a supervisor or employee), this model can be used as an instant identification of one's "Service-Leadership©" ability and directly drive the behaviors necessary to get into the top right quadrant.

The Bottom Left Quadrant guides both individual and group behaviors for peak performance.

Chapter Seven - *Understanding Your "Service-Leadership© Engagement Style" for Peak Performance*

Whether you are in management or at the frontline, understanding your own managerial leadership style will aid in the behaviors you exhibit. It is your behaviors that the customers experience, and it ultimately influences their actions and reactions to you.

Your managerial leadership style or tendencies is referred to as your "Service-Leadership©" style. It is your customer-focused engagement that either aids in attaining peak performance or ensures disaster.

There are four core "Service-Leadership©" styles that one can draw upon to facilitate the effective behavioral patterns that are expected from customer service professionals and lead to W.O.W.®!

To strategically design future initiatives to address market needs and facilitate growth, while at the same time addressing immediate tactical activities to do the "business of business," just ask your customers for their feedback in "product" and "service" areas.

This data will enable you to *fast-track* your activities for enhanced performance!

As detailed in the previous chapter for measuring customer views about an organization or individual, you can also use the same "L-Grid" instrument to determine your best course of "Service-Leadership© Engagement Style."

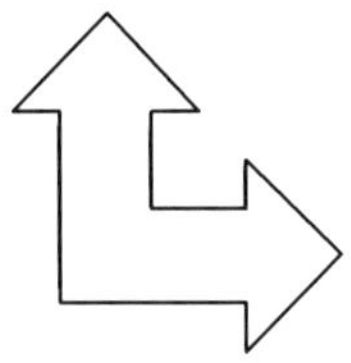

This data will enable you to *fast-track* short, intermediate and long-term activities for enhanced performance abilities and increased growth and profitability each day.

Whether you solicit this data verbally or via a manual instrument/survey for feedback, the vehicle doesn't matter. What matters is that you systematically, routinely and objectively solicit feedback from those customers that truly matter to your business.

Determine the best opportunities of engaging these core customers, where you would be most inclined to gather objective, thoughtful driven information as feedback that can be logically utilized.

What can skew this approach? The frustration to effective organizational dynamics is the volume of consultants with limited to no real workplace application experience. This is further compounded by an even larger number of professional speakers and consultants with limited to *no professional credentials* in areas they profess to be professionals!

Ask yourself, would you have your taxes done by an accountant that is not a CPA? Go to a medical doctor that is not board certified or engage an attorney that has not passed the bar exam? I believe your answer would be "no!" And, so too should be the measurement for the management consultant you read, follow or engage!

Don't be misled. You drive your management style/needs based upon the predetermined customer (internally or externally) feedback data. How to do so? Simple—solicit two sets of feedback responses from the ***Customer Service Index***. Where you dissect the "L-Grid" (vertical for product measurements and horizontal for personnel measurements) will determine which quadrant you will land.
This rating/information will:

1. Determine precisely how the customer measures and rates you.

2. Explains precisely how they feel about you.

3. Identify areas for improvement.

4. What management intervention style is internally and externally needed to recover or sustain success*.

5. And, whether or not that person will come back to you in the future.

***Your Customer Service Index© rating, tells a lot about your "Service-Leadership© Engagement Style!"**

How the customer rates you on the vertical and horizontal axis line, directly correlates to how you must act. *Their perception is everything*!

Your CSI© rating serves as an over-lay to another model for business performance improvement. The score on the CSI© tells a lot about you and determines actions that are appropriate.

The four quadrants of the CSI© also parallel the four quadrants imposed by the "Service-Leadership© Engagement Style" model (as first presented in ***YIELD MANAGEMENT: The Leadership Alternative To Performance and Net Profit Improvement***, by CRC Press/St. Lucie Press. ISBN# 1-57444-206-6 / USA $39.95, www.JeffreyMagee.com/library.asp).

How a customer scores the level of service they receive, also reveals which of the four management styles is best assumed by an organization's leadership. From a management perspective, recognize which quadrant your customer places you, and then recognize the corresponding Service-Leadership© approach to assume both externally with a customer and internally with an employee.

From a Service-Leadership© perspective, the same "L-Grid" axis lines represent powerful managerial information. The vertical axis will represent the "knowledge" level of an individual (customer or employee) and the horizontal axis line represents the "attitude" level of an individual (customer or employee). Consider these parallel instruments as a guidepost for action in attaining BEYOND W.O.W.® level interventions:

1. ***Bottom left quadrant—COUNSELOR Style.*** Your customer scores you as *"Poor Customer Care"* and implies that the customer feels that the product or goods, nor the service, individual, or people are meeting their acceptable needs and/or expectations. Immediate tough management intervention is warranted.

   External Application: As a counselor, this "Service-Leadership©" style implies that while you not become rude, you become

External Application: Assuming this engagement style dictates that you slow down while engaging the customer, become more patient and assess at what level the customer's present knowledge is on the issue that has brought the two of you together. The customer at this level needs education, training and information on the product or service at hand, which has placed them in the lower right quadrant in the CSI© model. This may mean either a hands-on, one-on-one approach or a need to direct them onward for further educational opportunities.

Internal Application: Assuming this role demands that you, as a Service-Leader, engage an employee demonstrating a positive and constructive "attitude" that is in need of "knowledge" and skill development and immediately design action plans like: classes, seminars, training programs, books, magazines, on going educational immersion opportunities through newsletter, magazines, journals, electronic newsletters (EZines), book-of-the-month clubs, etc., that will deliver the cutting edge information necessary for your personnel to remain as industry leaders.

4. ***Top right quadrant—MENTOR***. Ideally, your rating should be ***top right quadrant***, *"Exceptional Customer Care"*—***people and product exceed expectations***!

   External Application: To maintain this level of success, employees must feel appreciated, valued and believe in what they do. Management must work to foster and promote this behavior. When engaging the customer from this quadrant and in the "Service-Leadership©" style, you need to first ensure that the customer knows that you are there as a value-added resource. Merely availing yourself to them may be all that is necessary.

This style does not warrant direct interaction or even that you are proactive. Merely that you are viewed as the 'come to' person by the customer to maintain their performance standards as they see appropriate.

Internal Application: To maintain peak performance from your personnel assets, make sure that there are go-to people with the performance behaviors you desire available for them to study under and model from.

When individuals connect at every level of a business, the level of "Service-Leadership©" success and effectiveness is overwhelming.

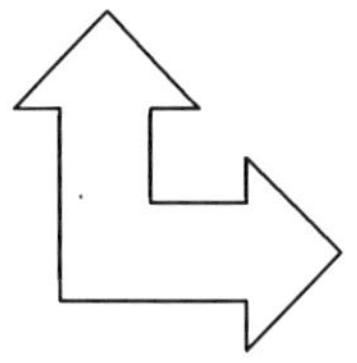

Again, by recognizing at which quadrant you fall into with this Service-Leadership© engagement model, you can instantly engage others. As a leader, coach your team to greatness, while at the same time guarding against micro management pitfalls….the power is in the "L-Grid!"

PART THREE – Turning Complaints into Profits:

Chapter Eight—
The Bottom Line Value of Complaints

Chapter Nine—
Creating a Service Recovery Plan

Chapter Ten—
Writing Complaint Response Letters that Bring Customers Back

Chapter Eleven—
Converting the Ballistic Customer into an Advocate Using the "ALWAYS Sandwich©" Angry Customers Engagement Formula

Chapter Twelve—
Golden Questions© for Minimizing Complaints and Growing Business

Chapter Eight -
The Bottom Line Value of Complaints

I came across a customer comment card recently for an interior design firm that read:

> **Please complain.**
>
> Thanks for your order. We want everything to go perfectly. If your order was late. Or wrong. Or if any of the goods were damaged in the slightest. Or if you're just having a lousy day and want to unload on someone—call our customer care hotline.

Why would a company encourage complaints? Put simply, it makes good business sense. Delivering truly outstanding service is clearly the goal of this interior design firm. The owner of this firm knows that 95% of the complaining customers will continue to do business if their problems are immediately resolved. They also knows that they **can't retain dissatisfied customers if they do not express their concerns**.

In our programs (seminars, retreats, keynotes, consultation, coaching), customer service professionals frequently tell me they don't like dealing with complaints and some say they don't particularly care for complaining customers. These responses to complaints are normal. Complaining customers can be difficult and the problems they experience can be complex. It's not always clear what to say and what to do.

But the fact is, we have to respond to complaints. Customers today are very much *value* oriented. When your customers buy your products or service, they expect a fair return on their investment. And when that doesn't happen, they have the right to tell you about it. As Service Leaders, we have a responsibility to listen and take action to correct the problem or clarify any misunderstandings. If we're smart, we'll respond to complaints in such a way that not only resolves the problem, but also completely restores the customer's confidence in the company and maintains their loyalty.

Earlier, we explained that customer service is a profit center. You should also know that complaint handling is actually a sales function with proven bottom line value. You've probably never thought of complaint handling as a sales function, but it certainly is. Every time you resolve a complaint and keep a customer from defecting to the competition, you have *sold* the company back to a customer who was on the brink of defection. Not only that, you have saved a tremendous amount of sales and marketing dollars. It costs four to six times more to replace a customer than it does to keep a customer.

Here are six specific reasons effective complaint handling adds net profit to the bottom line and should be viewed as a critical sales function.

1. **Builds Loyalty**. TARP, Inc. (Technical Assistance Research Programs) has found that 95% of complaining customers will remain loyal if their problems are resolved immediately. And it gets better: The same company's research revealed that the mere voicing of a complaint (even in the absence of resolution) increases loyalty by as much as 10%.

2. **Increases Sales**. Successfully regaining customer goodwill after service mishaps and maintaining loyalty at every service encounter boosts sales. Over time, loyal customers (the customers you successfully won back) tend to be willing to pay a premium price for your products or services. Research by Bain & Co. found that loyal customers are less price sensitive than new customers.

3. **Generates Positive Word-of-Mouth Advertising**. When service is truly outstanding, customers will tell an average of five people about the great service. If the service doesn't meet the customer's expectations, they will tell 11 people. But, if there's a problem and it is resolved immediately, customers will tell 17 people about the service recovery. Getting it right the first time, results in 5 people hearing the good news story. If your company blows it, but offers a quick recovery, you can generate more than three times as much positive word-of-mouth advertising.

4. **Decreases Acquisition Costs**. Most industry experts agree it costs four to six times more to win a new customer than it does to keep an existing customer. When you maintain loyalty after a mishap, you have just reduced acquisition costs.

5. **Reduces Problem Occurrence and Customer Dissatisfaction**. When complaint handling is done correctly, customer feedback is used to eliminate problems at the root and the data must be used to help the company anticipate and prevent future problems from occurring.

6. **A 5% increase in retention can lead to a net profit of 85% to the bottom line.** Generally, retaining just 5% more customers (who were

otherwise heading straight to the competition after a service mishap) will translate into a bottom line profit increase of 25% to 85%. See chapter 16 for a breakdown of this profit increase calculation.

Most Dissatisfied Customers Don't Complain

Clearly, we have a tremendous opportunity to increase profits when we effectively respond to complaints and maintain loyalty. However, the fact is, most dissatisfied customers do not complain. Research conducted by TARP, Inc. found that for every complaint a company receives, there are approximately 27 other customers with a problem who won't tell you about it. They will, however, spread negative word-of-mouth advertising to 11 people on average.

Don't let the numbers deceive you

When I worked in consumer affairs in the car rental industry, part of my job was to contact managers of below standard service locations and work with them to bring service to acceptable levels. I recall a conversation with one manager who became irritated (an understatement) that I would call him to talk about 32 complaints in a 30-day period. "*I rent 110 cars a day, everyday, and you're calling me because of 30 complaints in 30 days! That's nothing and clearly, you have NOTHING to do*!"

When you look at the raw numbers, 30 complaints in 30 days is not all that bad. But the raw numbers are just that – raw. (And, by the way, I had plenty tasks to keep me busy.) The fact is, and the point of my call to this manager, most dissatisfied customers won't complain. If every complaint received actually represents 27 dissatisfied customers, the impact of receiving 30 complaints in 30 days is more like this:

30 complaints
x27 mute unhappy customers
=810 Dissatisfied customers

This location, which serves more than 3000 customers a month, was blowing it with 810 customers a month, or nearly one-third of their customer base. And it gets worse. Unhappy customers will tell an average of 11 people each about their dissatisfaction. This is the one customer who complains to you and the 27 who don't ever tell you about the problem. Eight hundred ten times 11 equals 8,910. That's how many people have heard the bad news story about this location's service in just 30 days. Now, you tell me, was it worth this manager's time to listen to what I had to say?

If dissatisfied customers don't complain, you can't retain them The first step toward turning complaining customers into loyal customers is to get dissatisfied customers to complain. Dissatisfied customers are often silent, opting to switch brands rather than talk.

If customers are dissatisfied, why don't they complain?

Dissatisfied consumers have given the following reasons for not voicing their complaints to organizations:

- Don't know where/who to complain.
- Don't want a confrontation.
- Fear of retribution. (i.e. If I complain about my entrée, someone might spit in my drink.)
- It's easier for me to do business elsewhere than to complain to the company.
- Don't have time to make a phone call or write a letter of complaint.

- Fear of getting the run-around on the phone by being transferred to one customer service representative to another without resolution.

Getting Dissatisfied Customers to Talk to You

The Harvard Business Review recently reported that Maine Savings Bank in Portland found a creative way to get complaining customers to talk. They *pay* customers to complain. You read it right. They pay customers to complain. When customers voice complaints about their accounts, bank services or offer solutions for service improvement, Maine Savings Bank pays $1. The bank receives more than 500 letters annually from customers. For a mere $500 a year, Maine Savings Bank is getting creative and profitable ideas for improving service. They capture hundreds of complaints that would have otherwise gone unvoiced, and retain customers because they're now sharing their experiences and concerns.

Given the value of complaints and complaining customers, actively soliciting customer feedback should be a strategic goal of every company. Make it easy for your unhappy customers to complain, and they will reward you with continued brand loyalty.

The Bottom Line Value of Complaints.

By now, you're probably beginning to see that complaints add value to organizations, and perhaps, the *Please Complain* comment card makes more sense. The word "complain" has never had a positive meaning, and most people simply don't like to handle complaints. The word "complain" brings to mind a whining, ungrateful, nit-picking customer image, or the demanding, irate and unreasonable customer we've all experienced. Rarely do we look forward to complaints or complaining customers. However, you now know that customer feedback is much more than a disgruntled customer.

You now know . . .

Every time you let a dissatisfied customer vent, you have just increased loyalty 10%. (Because customers who complain—even in the absence of satisfactory resolution are more loyal than unhappy customers who don't complain.)

And . . .

Remember complainants who have their problems resolved immediately to their satisfaction will tell 17 people on average about your service recovery.

You also know that increasing customer retention by just 5%, can, in many cases, result in a net profit increase of 25% to 85%. When your company or your customer service department retains just 5% of complaining customers, you are adding substantial profits to the bottom-line.

Effective complaint handling really does add net profit to the bottom line. In chapter nine, we will examine the elements of developing a service recovery plan that will keep customers coming back again and again after any service mishap.

Chapter Nine -
Creating a Service Recovery Plan

The service recovery plan is your key to turning complaints into profits.

Given the fact that it costs four to six times more to win a new customer than to keep an existing customer and the significant profit potential of retaining just five percent[1] more of your customers, it only makes sense for the Service-Leader to design a service recovery plan that will position your company to keep more customers coming back, even after service mishaps.

In order to turn complaints into profits, you will need a solid service recovery plan. Without a service recovery plan, complaints become a hassle and create a hole in your purse. As a result, many of your complainants will ultimately defect to the competition. **A service recovery plan is a plan of action designed to completely restore customer confidence in your company and regain customer goodwill after service failures**.

The 10 Step Service Recovery Plan

Myra's Golden Rules: Years ago I headed up Consumer Affairs at Thrifty Rent-A-Car System. I led a strategic team of Customer Loyalty Advocates who had the critical responsibility of responding to questions and complaints. After working in Consumer Affairs for just a few months, I became concerned about the company's retention rate

[1] Frederick Riechheld, author of *The Loyalty Effect*, found that retaining just 5% more customers can result in a net profit increase to the bottom line of 25% to 85%.

among complainants. Were we retaining customers who complained, or were we simply resolving problems? My team was effective in responding to questions and resolving the issues and their overall performance effectiveness was good. But what mattered to me most was retaining the customer.

I suspected that the missing link in our customer interactions was not the logistics of problem resolution, but the way we spoke to our customers. So I went to work and developed a brand new dialogue for my people to use to frame their conversations with unhappy customers. I never wanted the conversation to sound scripted, and I wanted to make sure that our comments clearly communicated to customers that resolving problems and maintaining loyalty was our top priority.

What emerged was a focused dialogue based on ten points designed to solve the problem the customer experienced, and to completely restore the customer's confidence in our company. My employees began using this new dialogue with great success. We were not only solving problems, but customer satisfaction increased significantly and retention among complaining customers dramatically increased. Resolving problems became easier because there was never any guesswork in what to say to create calm, diffuse anger, and gain trust – the dialogue had it built in.

I later named the dialogue the ***10 Golden Rules for Complaint Resolution.*** The 10 Golden Rules formulate the perfect service recovery plan by restoring customer confidence in the company, completely regaining customer goodwill and certainly bringing customers back again and again. Service leaders and frontline professionals in hundreds of organizations and dozens of industries have now experienced the 10 Golden Rules in our workshops and can all testify to the ease and effectiveness of using this simple, yet creative dialogue to resolve complaints.

Here are the ***10 Golden Rules for Complaint Resolution.***

GOLDEN RULE #1: Express appreciation for the feedback. Expressing appreciation for feedback is as simple as saying, *"Thank you for taking the time to tell us about this. We appreciate customers who let us know when things aren't right."* Many customers will be shocked with your gratitude. All will remember you with goodwill.

GOLDEN RULE #2: Show empathy. Empathy can be a powerful tool used to disarm an angry customer and show that you genuinely care about the inconvenience the customer has experienced. Not to be confused with sympathy, empathy is identification with and understanding of the customer's situation and feelings. You can express empathy by saying something similar to, *'It must have been very frustrating for you to have experienced a delay in service. For that I am sorry.*"

GOLDEN RULE #3: Apologize. Research has found that when an apology is perceived as genuine, customer satisfaction increases 10% to 15%. An apology should be offered both when the company is responsible for the problem and when the company is not responsible. An apology does not have to be an admission of fault. For example, you might say, "*I'm so sorry for any misunderstanding you have experienced.*" Or *'If I were in your shoes, I'm* *sure I'd feel just as you do. I'm sorry for the frustration you have experienced.*"

GOLDEN RULE #4: Have a sense of urgency. Ninety-five percent of complaining customers will remain your customers if their problems are resolved immediately; Meaning, during that phone call. This is compared to only 70% when there is a delay in resolution. To maximize your opportunity to regain goodwill and keep the customer, you'll want to work with and demonstrate a sense of urgency. Make it clear that resolving the problem is as important to you as it is to the customer. You can demonstrate a sense of urgency with your words, tone and literally by moving quickly to resolve the problem.

GOLDEN RULE #5: Ask for necessary information. Notice that asking for information is step 5, not step 1. We defer asking for necessary information until after we have established rapport and begun to build trust with the customer. This helps avoid the perception that we're not allowing venting time and that our questioning is an interview or worse, an interrogation positioned to "prove" the customer wrong.

GOLDEN RULE #6: Assure the customer. Your customer may have the fear that their problem can't be solved or that *you* can't solve their problem. You can reduce anxiety by assuring the customer that together you'll get to the bottom of this. Say something similar to, "*I* *understand exactly what happened and we'll get this taken care of right away.*"

Additionally, customers want and need to know exactly what you are doing to correct the problem they've experienced. Ron Zemke, co-author of *Knock Your Socks Off Service Recovery* said in a recent article, *"It doesn't matter whether the problem was caused by the customer, by your company, by a third party, or an act of nature; the customer wants to know what you are doing to resolve the issue and get things back on track. That need for reassurance is tantamount."*

GOLDEN RULE #7: Tell the customer what you're going to do. Ron Zemke warns: *"It's a basic tenet of customer psychology. Problems, questions, and uncertainties weigh on their (customer's) minds. The more urgent the issues, the more important the resolution, the more feedback and information the customer wants and needs from you.*" It's terribly important to keep customers in the loop on the steps you're taking to resolve their problems. They expect and deserve to know how their situation is being resolved. For example, you might simply explain, *"I'll need to do some investigating on my end and speak with my manager about this. He is out of the office now but I expect him early this afternoon. I will call you back no later than 4 p.m. with a response."*

GOLDEN RULE #8: Solve the problem. Follow-up and resolve the problem as quickly as possible.

GOLDEN RULE #9: Ask, "Have we resolved the problem to your satisfaction?" Our idea of a resolution may not necessarily be the customer's idea of a satisfactory resolution. Ask your customer if you've met their expectations. If the answer is no, continue talking with the customer until you're sure you've met expectations or until you've offered a reasonable explanation for why you weren't able to satisfy them.

GOLDEN RULE #10: Investigate the problem and work to cut it at its root. This is the preventative step of complaint management. Research the problem to determine the root-cause and take proactive steps to eliminate the problem.

When Service Leaders respond to complaints with the 10 Golden Rules, it's easy to restore customer confidence in the company and quickly regain customer goodwill after service mishaps.

Empower and challenge your staff to make every unhappy customer want to come back and tell everyone they know about the service recovery.

A True Story of Outstanding Service Recovery at Thrifty Rent-A-Car System

When I was overseeing consumer affairs for Thrifty Rent-A-Car System we received an unusual complaint from a very unhappy customer. In a hurry to catch a flight after a magical day at Disneyland, the customer inadvertently left her son's 3-foot Mickey Mouse toy in the rental car. When the customer contacted Thrifty the next day, Mickey Mouse was nowhere to be found.

Jim took the call and instead of explaining (policy) that the company wasn't responsible for items left in vehicles, he got creative. He told the customer he'd do everything he could to locate Mr. Mouse. Just as the customer suspected, Mickey Mouse was missing in action. What did Jim do? He left work that day and went to the local Disney Store and bought a 3-foot Mickey Mouse and had the store ship it Fed-Ex to our customer. Talk about memorable! Do you think the customer wanted to come back to Thrifty? Do you think she told everyone she knew about the SERVICE RECOVERY? You bet she did! Jim's creativity resulted in a **customer for life** and priceless word-of-mouth advertising and cost the company less than 50 bucks!

Encourage your staff to leave each unhappy customer with a compelling drive to come back and tell others about the service recovery. Here are three more creative ideas Thrifty employees use to bring customers back and make them want to tell everyone they know…

1. One employee came up with the phrase, "*We're sorry we dropped the ball*" and gave us the creative idea of sending customers a softball with Thrifty's logo and Customer Care's toll free number on it. Customer Care began shipping the softball out with the "*We're sorry we dropped the ball*" letter to select upset customers.

2. Someone came up with the idea of sending customers a bouquet of flowers or box of chocolates after complaints were resolved as a further gesture of goodwill.

3. At one time every employee handwrote thank you notes to 25 complaining customers each week. The note thanked customers for taking the time to give the company their feedback.

Challenge your team to find creative ways to make each voiced complaint a memorable, loyalty-maintaining encounter. Strive to make every unhappy customer want to come back and want to tell everyone they know about your service recovery. When you do, you'll build customer loyalty and generate valuable word-of-mouth advertising.

Using Customer Feedback Strategically to Improve Processes

No service recovery is complete until you have strategically used the feedback from customers to make business improvements. Customer feedback must be captured, analyzed and disseminated. When you collect, analyze, and report your data with the focused purpose of contributing to long range planning, as well as problem solving, it can truly be a bottom-line benefit to your company.

Golden Rule # 10 *is investigate the problem and work to cut it at its root*. All top complaints need to go through a rigorous root-cause analysis process so you can reduce or eliminate the causes. The top ten complaints customers voice today should not be the same top ten complaints you hear this time next year. That's because you are monitoring complaints and taking aggressive measures to eliminate the root-causes of common problems.

A second way to use feedback more strategically is to share customer complaint data with key people within your organization so that customer-impacting changes can be made. Your frontline customer service professionals are privy to data that can help your organization cut costs and increase income…when that data is used. Customer feedback data needs to be disseminated to Training & Development, Research & Development, Field staff and managers, Sales & Marketing, and other key departments.

Always remember that a complete service recovery is more than resolving the problem the customer encountered, it is retaining the customers and using customer feedback strategically to learn from problems.

When you have a well-designed and well-implemented service recovery plan, it really is possible to turn complaints into profits by retaining customers who are on the brink of defection and using customer feedback data strategically to make process improvements. Service-Leaders respond to complaints with the *10 Golden Rules* and always look for ways to learn from feedback, and they find that most of their complaining customers remain their customers!

Chapter Ten
Writing Complaint Response Letters that Bring Customers Back

In this chapter, we reveal the Seven Golden Rules for Writing Complaint Response Letters, tips for responding to email complaints, and the four most common letter writing mistakes—and how to avoid them. When you complete this chapter, you will be equipped to quickly generate sincere, complete complaint response letters that restore customer confidence in your company after service mishaps have occurred.

Four Deadly Mistakes Companies Make When Writing Response Letters

1. Sending out a "canned" letter—An airline passenger found a roach in his salad. Upon arriving at his hotel that evening he immediately wrote an angry letter to the airline. By the time he returned to his office from the business trip, a reply from the airline awaited him.

The letter read "*Dear Sir: Your letter caused great concern to us. We have never before received such a complaint and pledge we will do everything within our power to insure such an incident will never happen again. It might interest you to know that the employee serving you has been reprimanded and the entire plane is being fumigated. Your concern has not fallen on deaf ears.*"

Needless to say, the man was impressed. Then he noticed an interoffice memo inadvertently stuck to the back of his letter with this message: *'Send this character the regular roach letter.*"

"Canned" or form letters, while convenient, are not well received by customers. If you choose to use form letters, use them as templates and take the time to customize each letter to specifically address the customer's situation.

2. **Giving a Delayed Response** - The speed of the response can have more of an impact on future loyalty than the actual resolution itself. TARP, Inc. found that 95% of dissatisfied customers experiencing minor problems will remain loyal if their complaints are resolved immediately. That number drops to 70% if the resolution is not immediate.

3. Failing to Mirror Emotional Content of Letters - If your best friend writes you a six page letter describing her man troubles, financial woes, career blues, her disgust with her weight, etc, would you write her back a two paragraph canned response? Of course you wouldn't! That would be an insult and you'd jeopardize your future relationship with this "best" friend. Customers are our friends too. When an unhappy customer takes the time to type up a two page, single-spaced letter of complaint, we insult them when we respond with a one or two paragraph "standard complaint" letter.

Regaining goodwill is not just about solving the problem it's about showing that you care, expressing empathy and connecting with the customer. Mirror customer letters by writing response letters that pace the length and emotion of the customer's letter. (This does not mean you have to send an eight-page letter to a customer who complains line by line for eight pages. It does mean your letter needs to be carefully thought out and structured and at least a full page with serious loyalty-regaining content.)

4. Sounding As If You Don't Want to Be Contacted - I recently contacted my utility company via email about a problem with my bill. The company's response was prompt and the representative's email ended with this statement:

"Please don't hesitate to reply or call me if you have any questions."

And the representative's name, email address and phone number was included in the email signature. It was clear that this company was *available* to me, should I have any further questions. But this isn't the case with all companies. I have received response letters from companies that actually did not include a contact name or number. The letter simply "ended." This is never acceptable and customers get your message loud and clear. Always leave the door open for customers who do not perceive the situation as resolved or simply have more questions.

Writing Response Letters That Restore Customer Confidence In the Company

Two years ago at Myra Golden Seminars, we experimented with changing our primary company color from royal blue to lime green. We tested client reaction to the idea by desktop printing all workbooks, handouts and promotional materials in the new color during all of our spring seminars. After the first test of the new color scheme I received this email from a participant of my Loyalty Advantage *seminar.*

From: *Lorena Boese*
To: *Myra Golden*
Subject: *Feedback*
Date: *May 1, 2001; 9:03 AM*

I found the print on your workbook hard to read. Those of us over 40 sometimes have difficulty reading certain fonts and colors and I had a hard time following your information and I think I missed out on important tips. Perhaps a darker color, like black or blue would be easier.

My ego was a bit bruised as green is my favorite color and the change to lime green was, of course, my idea. But the whole point of testing the color was to make sure it was a good move before *committing. My client's feedback was valuable in helping us make our decision. I personally wrote the response email, following the Golden Rules and here it is:*

From: *Myra Golden*
To: *Lorena Boese*
Subject: *Feedback*
Date: *May 1, 2001; 9:49 AM*
*(*response sent within one hour of receiving complaint*)*

*Thank you for your feedback on our seminar workbooks. We appreciate customers who take the time to tell us how we can better serve them. (*Expressing appreciation for feedback*) It must have been terribly frustrating for you to sit through our seminar and not be able to take full advantage of the workbook. (*Showing empathy for the inconvenience the customer experienced.*)*

Please accept my sincere and unreserved apology for the inconvenience you experienced in not being able to easily follow the outline in the workbook. (Offering sincere apology) *Would you believe we usually do use only black and blue fonts? This spring we're testing a new color scheme to see how clients will respond. Your feedback will prove invaluable as we sit down and decide whether or not to move forward with the change. We will immediately send you a new workbook with black print. We will ship that today.* (Telling customer what we're going to do/responding with a sense of urgency.)

Ms. Boese, I'm eager to restore your confidence in our company and regain your goodwill. As a concrete form of apology, I am also sending you a disk with my PowerPoint presentation. (Adding something to the resolution, as a gesture of goodwill.) *You can share these slides with your co-workers, employees, and bosses so everyone can work together creatively and strategically to develop a service strategy that makes customers love you, come back again and again and tell everyone they know.*

Please email me or call me if I have not completely regained your goodwill. (Invite customer to stay in touch if not satisfied.) *Thanks for attending yesterday's seminar and thank you for your valuable feedback on our workbook print.*

Myra Golden
Principal, Myra Golden Seminars
866-873-8419
myra@myragolden.com

By the way, my partner and I decided to stay with the royal blue print for our logo and materials. He never liked the idea of lime green, and I knew if one customer had a problem with it, there were likely 20 to 30 other people who found it frustrating but chose not to say anything.

Responding to complaints received by letter is no different than responding to complaints by phone. You'll want to respond with a sense of urgency, personalize the response, express empathy, offer a sincere apology and ensure customer satisfaction. In my letter writing labs, I give participants the Golden Rules for Complaint Resolution (Chapter 9) as a template and have them develop written responses as carefully as they would verbal responses based on the Golden Rules.

The 7 Golden Rules for Writing Complaint Response Letters

I quickly drafted the email in the example above using the "Seven Golden Rules for Writing Complaint Letters." The rules are simple, make letter writing easy, and successfully regain customer goodwill after a service mishap. Before sending out any written response to letters or emails, go through the 7 Golden Rules and make sure you've covered all of the bases.

1. ***Express appreciation for feedback*** - A lot of companies begin complaint response letters with: "We have received your letter dated..." Don't do this. The fact that you're responding to the letter is irrefutable proof that you have received the customer's letter. Instead of wasting words, immediately go into a response designed to restore the customer's confidence and regain their goodwill.

My favorite approach to beginning a complaint letter is to begin by expressing appreciation for the feedback.

Here are some ways to express appreciation for customer feedback:

- ✍ *"Thank you for taking the time to write to us."*

- ✍ *"Thank you for your letter. We appreciate customers who let us know when things aren't right."*

- ✍ *"Thank you so much for taking the time to write to us. We appreciate the opportunity to clarify what we think has happened."* (This is ideal for a response letter to a customer who is actually responsible for the error or when you cannot honor the customer's request for a refund or exchange.)

2. Show empathy - If you've participated in one of our seminars, you've no doubt heard me preach on the value of empathy. Empathy can be a powerful tool used to disarm an angry customer and show that you genuinely care about the inconvenience the customer has experienced. Not to be confused with sympathy, empathy is identification with and understanding of the customer's situation and feelings.

You can express empathy by saying something similar to, "It must have been very frustrating for you to have waited five days for your order and for that I am sorry."

3. **Apologize -** Make a note of this rule: <u>Never send out a response letter without an apology</u>. Never.

Research has found that when an apology is perceived as genuine, customer satisfaction increases 10% to 15%. An apology should be offered both when the company is responsible for the problem and when the company is not responsible. An apology does not have to be an admission of fault. For example, you might say, *"I'm so sorry for any misunderstanding you have experienced." Or "If I were in your shoes, I'm sure I'd feel just as you do. I'm sorry for the frustration you have experienced."*

4. **Respond with a sense of urgency** (This includes both responding immediately and expressing a sense of urgency about regaining goodwill.)

Ninety-five percent of complaining customers will remain your customer if their problems are resolved immediately. Immediately, meaning that visit or that phone call. This is compared to only 70% when there is a delay in resolution. To maximize your opportunity to regain goodwill and keep the customer, you'll want to work with and demonstrate a sense of urgency. Make it clear that resolving the problem is as important to you as it is to the customer. You can demonstrate a sense of urgency with your words, tone and literally by moving quickly to resolve the problem.

In the example response email, I demonstrated a sense of urgency at two points:

A. "We will immediately send you a new workbook with black print. We will ship that today."

B. "Ms. Boese, I'm eager to restore your confidence in our company and regain your goodwill. As a concrete form of apology, I am also sending you a disk with my PowerPoint presentation."

5. **Tell the customer what you're going to do -** Clearly explain to the customer exactly what you plan to do to resolve the problem. This is especially important if the resolution will take some time.

6. **Give them double for their trouble (Add a goodwill token like a coupon or a complimentary product) -** In my email to Ms. Boese, I did this with this statement: *"I am also sending you a disk with my PowerPoint presentation.*" Sometimes in complaint resolution, it is appropriate to add a little something to the recovery to ensure customer goodwill. This can be as simple as a coupon inviting the customer to come back and try your product or service at a discount. It won't always be necessary to make it a double for their trouble but doing this can help maintain and strengthen loyalty.

7. **Invite customers to contact you if they aren't satisfied -** Make it easy for your customers to contact you if they need more information. Always give your name, toll-free number, email address and website.

When you respond to complaint letters and emails using the 7 Golden Rules, your letters will be customized, sincere and professional and they will not only deliver a resolution, but will facilitate your restoring the customer's confidence in the company and maintaining customer loyalty.

Response Time Guidelines

A question I'm frequently asked is "*What is a reasonable response time for complaint letters*?" The answer: **The faster, the better**. Research by TARP, Inc. found that organizations can increase loyalty after a complaint if:

1. The customer receives an immediate reply acknowledging letter.
2. The customer receives satisfactory resolution within two weeks.

I know it isn't always feasible to resolve complaints immediately, either because the resolution requires research or because operations responsibilities do not afford you the time to respond to letters as promptly as you would like. When you're not able to respond with a resolution within two to three days, simply send out an initial reply immediately upon receiving the customer's letter. When I was overseeing consumer affairs, here's the letter I created for my staff to use when resolution couldn't be immediately offered:

Thank you so much for taking the time to write to us. Your letter has been forwarded to (responsible representative's name) and you can expect a reply within ten business days. Should you need to reach us sooner, please contact (responsible representative) directly at 1-800-000-0000 x 000.

This simple letter allowed us to stay in communication with customers without causing a breakdown in workflow during peak volume times.

Responding to Email Complaints

In 1999, when I was heading up Consumer Affairs at Thrifty, we realized more than a 300% increase in complaints via email over 1998. The trend continued in 2000 with a 264% increase over the previous year. We were scrambling to keep up, as postal mail and phone complaints did not decrease. We discovered that customers who voiced complaints by email were a new group of customers. This was a group of customers that probably wasn't likely to complain if it were not for the convenience of being able to sit at a computer at 3 a.m. and sending a note of complaint. Many of these complaints were minor, most not even disputing a dollar amount. But they were complaints, and we had to respond.

At that time, Thrifty had a goal of resolving all complaints that came by mail within ten business days. As a trailblazing e-commerce consumer myself, I knew that a ten-day response to email complaints was definitely taboo. So I did a little survey to benchmark what other corporate customer care departments were doing. I contacted ten companies by email with a complaint in order to test their speed of response. The companies represented included a large manufacturer of home computers, an international hotel chain, a restaurant, cellular phone company, a bookstore, and of course, a car rental company. (In order to protect the guilty, I won't reveal the company names.) Of the ten companies, only one responded immediately. The cellular phone company sent an automatic response within minutes and a detailed answer in less than ten hours. The computer manufacturing company responded 28 days later and not one of the other eight companies even bothered to respond! My survey told me that many companies are **failing** customers miserably and that *any* effort I took would take Thrifty to the top of the game.

E-commerce experts seem to agree that an immediate response is expected for all email inquiries—**immediate being within the hour**—and the final answer/resolution must be given within two business days. According to recent research by Jupiter Research, only one-third of companies bother to immediately acknowledge they received a customer's email by sending an automatic response. In Jupiter's research, most companies did eventually respond, but only 52% did so within 24 hours and 32% took three days or longer, or did not respond at all. Research shows that 59% of high-spending consumers (those who spend more than $500 online over six months) expect a resolution to an email inquiry within 24 hours.

It's important for companies to meet customers' expectations for email response, otherwise your customers may initiate communication via more expensive means—live operators, postal mail, etc. Or worse, your customers may defect to the competition and spread negative word-of-mouth advertising.

Seven Simple Guidelines for Responding to Email Queries

1. Check emails as frequently as you check the phones. You answer the phones every time they ring and emails should be treated the same way. It's not acceptable to check customer emails one or two times daily or hourly. Email response must be a priority.

2. Send an initial reply immediately. The easiest and most economical means for an initial reply is to have an automatic reply setup through your complaint tracking system or other software package. Some software packages are sophisticated enough to read the customer's email, pick up on key words and reply based on email content. Other, simpler, packages simply respond with content you input. At Thrifty, we simply said:

Thank you for contacting us. Your email has been forwarded to our Customer Care Department. We will contact you within two business days.

3. Reply via email. Customers contacting you by email are suggesting that email is their preferred method of communication. Unless absolutely necessary, avoid calling or sending a response via postal mail. (Obviously, refunds or token items would still be sent postal mail.)

4. Resolve problem within 48 hours. The sooner the better. Email customers do not have tolerance for a 3-5-day turnaround. Strive for immediacy.

5. Activate the spell-check feature. Spelling counts. Always, always proof emails.

6. Capture and archive emails in your CRM system. It's critically important to log all email communications (both to and from the company) in your customer relationship management (CRM) system with dates and times. This helps you when emails are escalated, information is misinterpreted or there is an accusation of no response from the company.

7. Post a FAQ section on your company's Contact Us page. Identify the top ten reasons customers email your company and post responses to these queries on your website. Doing this can reduce the number of emails coming into your department or can better prepare your staff to respond. For example, At Thrifty Rent-A-Car System, hundreds of customers contact Customer Care each month requesting a copy of a past rental agreement. The Customer Care Department has created a form on the website specifically for customers requesting a rental agreement. Amazon.com has forecasted dozens of FAQ customers are likely to encounter and listed them on their site.

Four Quick Letter Writing Tips:

1. **Quickly get to the point**. Customers await responses from companies with great anticipation. Don't use your response letter as an opportunity to promote products or services. And by all means, don't waste words. Simply express appreciation for the feedback, apologize for the problem and quickly offer your resolution strategy or explanation.
2. **Tell the customer what you *can* do**. Even when you can't give the customer exactly what they're asking for, you should make every offer to help them. Make a point to emphasize what you can do for your dissatisfied customer rather than what you cannot do. When you give your customers options and clearly work to help them, you're much more likely to regain customer goodwill and maintain the customer's loyalty.
3. **Keep Sentences Short**. A good average sentence length for business correspondence is in the range of 14 to 20 words. Readability studies show that people can quickly comprehend a 20-word sentence and move on to the next thought. A 30-word sentence causes them to slow down, however, and a 40-word sentence may require rereading.
4. **Avoid Jargon**. Make sure your letter doesn't contain acronyms or terms not easily interpreted. All customer correspondence needs to be simple and crystal clear.

Responding to complaint letters doesn't have to be difficult. Make sure your responses are sent out immediately, that they mirror the customer's pace and emotions, and always follow the Seven Golden Rules.

When you follow our simple letter generating process, you will find that your letters not only resolve problems, but they also restore the customer's confidence in your company and regain goodwill.

Chapter Eleven - *Converting the Ballistic Customer Into An Advocate Using The "ALWAYS Sandwich©" Angry Customers Engagement Formula*

The stories abound relating to every customer that comes to you upset and there can be many more just like them that are not coming forth. And those that don't come forth cannot be engaged and satisfied. Satisfied customers are more inclined to be repeat customers than an upset customer will be.

Some surveys indicate as many as eleven (Rule 1/11) other customers can have like discrepancies (FORUM Corp. research) with you and will not tell you, for every one that actually comes forward. And compounding this are estimates and varying surveys that also indicate that for every one upset customer that you have, that comes to you and leaves still upset due to lack of attention and engagement, they may tell upwards of two dozen (Rule 1/24) other people of their perceived horrific experience with "you!"

Rule 1/11 and Rule 1/24 Can Work Against Your Organization, and Rule 1/0 Can Grow You!

Engaging an upset customer, maintaining control of that conversation and striving for a healthy resolution is the challenge. With a controlled engagement approach, success can be attained more often than not. Converting an initially upset customer into an advocate can become a norm. Some surveys indicate by doing this you greatly increase the retention of the customer and decrease greatly the likelihood that they may feel compelled to share anything unflattering about you with others (Rule 1/0). In fact, they may even share with those closest to them the positive outcome you bestowed upon them!

So, converting that ballistic or upset customer into one which you can engage and address their needs, in an attempt to keep them as a customer, is both an art and a science.

Psychology reveals that what may have caused a customer to attain the level of negativity which they are exhibiting is caused by typically three factors:

1. A feeling or belief that they are not being *ACKNOWLEDGED.* Thus, to get acknowledged, they must exhibit an otherwise undesirable behavioral pattern.

2. A feeling or belief that no one will assume *OWNERSHIP* of their issue, and that they are being passed off from one contact to another. Thus to get someone to take ownership, they must exhibit an otherwise undesirable behavioral pattern.

3. A feeling or belief that nothing will be DONE on the issue being raised to the service provider. Thus to get anything done/fixed/resolved, they must exhibit an otherwise undesirable behavioral pattern.

So given this powerful insight, your engagement approach for ballistic and upset customers should chronologically speak to each of these psychological motivators. The "ALWAYS Sandwich© Angry Customers" Formula allows you to do precisely this – whether face-to-face, one-on-one, in group dynamics, via email and correspondence or over the telephone.

The "ALWAYS" acronym and portion of the formula serves as the first engagement step and allows you to simply create a conducive engagement environment to get all of the players involved to engage civilly.

Using the letters of the acronym, you facilitate a dialogue and manage your behavior in a very controlled and systematic manner.

STEP ONE Engagement Approach = ALWAYS:

1. **A** = **Apologize** in an emphatic manner and transition into a Q&A sequence.

2. **L** = **Listen** intently to the customer and increase your comprehension by physically taking notes of the key items for action response. This also decreases your ability of interrupting them and escalating emotions.

3. **W** = **Write down** only the key items for your response. Omit all of the superficial elements and emotion-based subject matter. Resolution of the customer complaint is the primary objective and a victory over name-calling is not.

4. **A** = **Apologize** again as you now transition from listening to them to now responding calmly to them. This second apology statement serves as a transition phase and also sends a signal to them that you are ACKNOWLEDGING what they have brought to your attention. You are also assuming OWNERSHIP of what they have presented, and

now you wish to present to them your position as to what can be DONE to address their concerns.

5. **Y = Your Name** should be immediately used in a way that, as you begin to respond, they hear someone has assumed OWNERSHIP for them and ensuring you will work with them. This will begin to powerfully diffuse any possible escalation in negativity and reduce continued tension between them and create more of an "us" mentality.

6. **S = Summarize** their points now in the conversational response flow and detail ways to address what they have brought to you.

The ALWAYS portion of the "ALWAYS Sandwich Angry Customers" Formula may sound like this, as a script:

1. ALW(ays) = "I am sorry that you have had the situation that you have mentioned, please tell me exactly what happened, let me take notes while you explain, and then let's see how we can address this for you."

2. (alw)AYS = "Based upon what you have detailed for me, there are a few ways we can proceed. Let me explain…"

In responding to the ballistic or upset customer, you now marry this first step with the second step, which is the SANDWICH part of the over-all formula.

By taking detailed mental and physical notes, you can now respond (SUMMARIZE) by taking everything that you have gathered and rebuild it into a smooth conversational flow, as if you were laying out all of the necessary ingredients before you to build a sandwich to eat.

STEP TWO Engagement Approach = SANDWICH:

1. POSITIVE - Start your response with something that you can immediately address, take action, resolve, and eliminate, etc. (Your base piece of bread in this sandwich analogy as the first ingredient to your response.)

2. NEGATIVE – Then, transition onward to that piece which may be laden with controversy, negativity or unpleasant. (The middle piece of response to this sandwich analogy.)

3. POSITIVE - End with or on a positive note. Transition immediately after matter-of-factly addressing the negative or middle portion of the dialogue (whether verbal or written) onward to a positive item. And if there are no items uncovered in your questioning and note-taking phase of this interaction that can be used as a positive ending, then end with a simple question that solicits more business. (... "Outside of this item, is there anything else we can be doing for you?")

The SANDWICH response portion of the "ALWAYS Sandwich© Angry Customers" formula may sound like this, as a script:

1. POSITIVE - "In looking at these items, one thing that we can immediately do to address this is to, ________________."

2. NEGATIVE - "In looking at this item, we are precluded by ________, and although I would like to do something, as you can see we cannot."

3. POSITIVE - "On this other item we may also be able to do something here, may I ask you a few additional questions, ___________?"

4. Alternative POSTITIVE - "Outside of these first two items, is there anything else we can do for you today?"

If the upset customer feels compelled after attempting a conversational flow with the SANDWICH formula, to digress back to the second ingredient where you attempted to dispense with the negative feelings, your response should be that of a smooth broken record. Replay the precise controlled, professional response you gave them the first time.

Customer Perception and Problem Situations

Most customers have low expectations when they give a company feedback. The way they see it, it's the company *against* them. From the customer's perspective, which is based on untold poor experiences with companies and complaints, it's as if there's a large brick wall placed in the center of the floor. On one side of the wall is the dissatisfied customer, who has experienced a problem, and on the other side of the wall, is the company. The problem the customer has experienced is on the same side of the wall as the company. From where the customer stands, it appears that the company is defending the problem (by quoting policy, placing blame, giving excuses etc.) and the two are joined together *against* the customer. This, of course, isn't how companies set out to make customers feel. It is, however, perception, and **perception is reality,** when it comes to our customers. This is the only perception that matters from the customer's perception.

Given the customer's perception of companies and service providers in problem situations, it's no small wonder that some customers will respond with anger and explosive verbal attacks when they feel they have been wronged.

The Reality of Problem Situations

Customers are right to think there is a barrier present in complaint situations. However, the situation is *not* the company defending the problem and working against the customer. On one side of the barrier, and let's call this barrier a fence instead of a wall, is the customer. On the other side of the fence is the problem. The company is standing on the same side of the fence as the customer, not with the problem. The company and customer are actually standing face to face, and they work together—communicating, brainstorming, and finding win-win solutions. The problem is the *problem*. The problem is not the customer. The problem is not the company. Yet many customers walk away from complaint situations feeling they are the problem and that the company's only objective was to "protect" policy.

Customers must feel you are their advocates, not adversaries. When customers feel you are their advocates, it is much easier to diffuse anger, reach win-win resolutions and maintain the customer's loyalty. The next two sections offer field-tested strategies for responding to ballistic customers in such a way that not only diffuses anger, but it also ensures that customers feel that the company is on their side throughout the problem resolution process.

Using the Principles of the Martial Art "Aikido" to Calm a Ballistic Customer

In my Customer Recovery programs, we demonstrate the martial art, Aikido, with a volunteer and then encourage participants to begin to practice "Verbal Aikido" with ballistic, demanding, and unreasonable customers. The martial art Aikido can be used to help customer Service Leaders more confidently and effectively respond to ballistic customers. Aikido students are taught to blend with the other person's energy so that energy doesn't knock them over and then to channel that energy into the direction they choose. Aikido is unique in that it is a non-violent martial art that never meets force with force. Using six principles of Aikido, customer service professionals can diffuse anger and demonstrate amazing control over all aspects of verbal attacks from demanding, irate, or unreasonable customers.

1. An Aikidoist strategically calms down the attack. This is done by both the use of relaxed body posture and open hands. Verbal attacks from irate customers also need the same calming strategy. In Aikido, the master will step aside rather than confront the attack. This takes the power and speed out of the attack and allows the master to stay centered and calm. When you respond to your customer with "*Clearly, we've upset you and getting to the bottom of this is just as important to me as it is to you,*" anger begins to dissipate. You've addressed the anger directly and non-defensively. You haven't been pulled into the drama of the attack.

2. Aikido never meets force with force. In fact, there are no direct attacks and very little striking or kicking. When dealing with angry customers it is natural to respond to an attack with an attack. If the customer yells, we escalate our voice. When the attack gets personal, we become defensive and less willing to work with the customer. While we may feel justified in launching our attack because we've been attacked, we must realize that a defensive (forceful) response only escalates the original problem. Let's learn from the Aikido masters and not attack back *defensively*. Instead, we will respond carefully and strategically.

3. Aikido emphasizes quick, decisive movements that are designed to use the attacker's force against him. This is done through evasive movements, body shifting, and leverage. Taking this to a verbal level, you'd take a customer's intensity and sense of urgency and use that to your advantage with a reply like: "*No question, we've messed up. Getting to the bottom of this is just as important to me as it is to you.*" Instead of letting the customer's intimidation tactics negatively impact you, you turn that energy back at the customer by pacing his actions.

4. Aikido's blend with their opponent's energy. In Aikido, this looks as if you move toward your opponent and then change places with them. In a verbal attack, blending with your customer is finding common ground with the customer. You can blend with your angry customer by listening with a sincere intent to understand their pain, frustration and needs and then responding with empathy. The knowledge you gain from listening to your customer becomes your force and positions you to redirect the energy in a productive direction. Once you've blended with the customer, that is, once you truly understand the customer's situation, the attack can be neutralized and redirected.

5. Aikido students learn to turn with their opponent's force and let that force go past them. When we respond to angry customers in this way, we're able to keep our cool when customers get hot. We don't get caught up in the emotion of anger. Instead, we allow the customer to express his feelings, and we don't take comments personally. We don't allow our feelings (anger, rejection, offense) to control our responses.

6. In Aikido, all opponents are considered partners. Think of your angry customer as your partner, and let this mindset direct you to use interactive dialogue to work *with* your customer to solve the problem. Try to not resist or coerce your "partner." Work with your partner, talk with your partner, and seek solutions that benefit the customer and the company.

Applying the principles of Aikido to difficult situations with ballistic customers allows Service Leaders to maintain composure and control, and effectively diffuse anger.

Five Ways to Influence Customer Behavior in Tough Situations

When dealing with the ballistic customer, it never hurts to be skilled in the art of persuasion. In 1936, Dale Carnegie wrote *How to Win Friends and Influence People* to "*help readers get along with and influence people in everyday, business and social contacts.*"

In the *How to Win People to Your Way of Thinking* section, Carnegie offers creative and practical strategies for responding to complaints by learning how to effectively use influence. Using influence with upset customers is not to manipulate customers or to present an insincere response. It is instead, knowing exactly what not to do and say and what to do and say. Here's a brief summary of Carnegie's pointers for influencing and winning customers to our way of thinking in complaint situations.

1. Realize you can't win an argument with your customer.

Certainly, you can prove your point and even have the last word, "*you may be right, but as far as changing your customer's mind is concerned, you will probably be just as futile as if you were wrong.*" Your goal in complaint situations is to retain the customer, not to be right. If you win the argument, you may very well have lost the customer. Carnegie encourages us to carefully consider some hard questions before going to battle with customers: "*Is my reaction one that will relieve the problem, or will it just relieve frustration? Will my reaction drive my customer further away? What price will I pay if I win (the argument)?*" Carnegie advises, "*The only way to get the best of an argument is to avoid it.*" By the way, customers will spread negative word-of-mouth advertising to 50 people if they get into argument with you!

2. Apologize for your mistakes.

We cannot emphasize enough the importance of apologizing to customers in problem situations and especially when customers demonstrate a "ballistic" temperament. In a recent consumer survey, 50% of customers who voiced complaints to an organization said they never received an apology. If the company is wrong, admit it quickly and emphatically. This will help you disarm your angry customer and reduce defensiveness. We also encourage customer service professionals to apologize even when they are not at fault. An apology does not have to be an admission of fault. It can be offered to express regret. For example, "*I'm so sorry for any inconvenience this misunderstanding has caused you.*"

3. Never tell a customer they are wrong.

You will be smart to never tell a customer s/he is wrong or mistaken. Telling a person they are wrong arouses opposition and will make the customer want to battle with you. (Ever tell your spouse they are wrong?) Carnegie points out an indisputable fact, "*It's difficult, under even the most benign conditions to change people's minds.*" So why make it harder by starting out on the wrong foot? If you know your customer is wrong, it's better to start off saying, "*I thought the contract read otherwise, but let's take a look.*"

4. Begin in a friendly way – you catch more bees with honey.

Avoid starting out on the defense or speaking with an authoritative tone as if you have to prove the customer wrong. Even when the customer is wrong, this is not an appropriate response. Beginning in a friendly way means hearing the customer out, allowing venting time and showing respect, even when your final answer is no.

5. Get a yes, yes response.

When talking with your customer, begin by emphasizing the things on which you agree. Dale Carnegie urges us to get the person saying yes and keeping them, if possible, from saying "no." When a person says "no," all of their pride demands that they remain consistent with themselves. The diplomatic communicator builds a psychological path toward an affirmative response by strategically getting their "opponent" to say "yes" a number of times. For example, you could approach a situation this way: "*Sir. You signed and agreed to the terms of the agreement and are, therefore, responsible for…*" This statement, while true, will certainly only incite an already upset customer. A more diplomatic approach might start this way: "*Would it be fair to say that you signed and accepted this contract?" (Yes.) And do you agree that when one signs a contract, it becomes a legal and binding document?*" (Yes.) What you've done here is brought your customer to a rational agreement with you and from here you can move into problem solving.

Your goal in problem situations with ballistic customers (or any customer for that matter) is not to be right and not to just resolve the problem, but to have everyone feel better about the problem that occurred and to **KEEP THE CUSTOMER**. The principles of Aikido and the five strategies presented here will help you do just that.

Most upset customers have been conditioned by previously ineffective customer service providers that, if they beat them up enough, others would capitulate. As a "Service-Leader" you are not going to play by these old corrosive behaviors.

The "Service-Leader" engages the customer, rather happy or upset, and collaboratively engages them for resolution and lasting transactions and success!

Chapter Twelve -

Golden Questions© for Minimizing Complaints and Growing Business

Converting every customer interaction, whether based upon a complaint or merely a routine interaction, into a business growth opportunity lies in your ability to frame and ask a Golden Question©.

Again, remember that psychology has learned that an upset or angry customer wants three basic needs to be addressed, and your Golden Questions should address these. This customer wants:

1. Someone to acknowledge their position and frustrations.
2. Someone to take ownership and address their concern and not pass them onto someone else or abdicate responsibility.
3. And, they want someone to take action on their needs!

Many businesses have been innovators and practitioners of the Golden Question© concept. And, just as the concept has been a catalyst to significant business growth opportunities and attributed to the building legions of loyal customers, the routine and insincerity in the questioner has also been the reason for these same businesses later demise or erosion in market share.

A ***"Golden Question©"*** by nature does three very important things:

1. It is framed with positive intent.

2. It solicits opportunities for additional business, whether that be in an up sale, cross sale or add on sale transaction.

3. It creates a positive impression in the customer's mind and creates an opportunity for future business interactions and desire by the customer to come back in the future when what they need is offered by you.

McDonald's Hamburger Restaurants is an innovator in the art and science of the "Golden Question©," although they too (as has become the case with all fast food restaurants today) have forgotten significant business growth opportunities by no longer aggressively using the concept. We have become a complacent world of order takers when it comes to engaging both the upset customer and the traditional customer transaction.

Imagine that you drive up to the drive-in order bay at such a restaurant today and order, from the picture-gram, a meal combo. No matter what item you order, what is the normal "Golden Question©" that customer service contact will ask?

Of course, "Would you like to super size your order?"

Whether you say yes or no, that customer service contact really sounds like they could care less, and thus that influences your response more often than not. Now, imagine that you owned that store. What could be the endless list of appropriate other "Golden Questions©" that the customer service contact could be asking? Also, frame them in a chronological order, to increase the opportunity for significant business growth opportunities.

In this situation, there are no less than five other "Golden Questions©" and multiple variations of each that could be asked with the patron ordering a simple picture-gram meal combo!

And by framing obvious add-on, up sale and cross sale "Golden Questions©" practically every customer engagement can be converted into an increased revenue stream of opportunities. You further satisfy your customer and increase your net profit from what would have been lost revenue opportunities!

Recently, I had my carpet cleaned by a company that obviously understands the value of asking "Golden Questions©." While engrossed in the laborious work of cleaning my carpet, one of the cleaning technicians asked, "*Have you ever noticed the gray dust buildup around your baseboards? That's a real good indicator that it's time to have your ducts cleaned.*"

She went on to explain that having my air ducts cleaned actually helps keep my carpet cleaner. This question was framed with positive intent, certainly solicited additional business, and you bet, the company created in me a desire to bring them back for an additional service I never before thought about, but now believed I NEEDED. The strategy worked, and I did bring them back at a later date for air duct cleaning.

This cleaning company asked not one, but two "Golden Questions©." The second "Golden Question©" came shortly before the crew finished the carpet cleaning job. The same technician observed my busy three year-old in high gear and she commented, "*I notice you have a toddler. If she's anything like my kids, you have lots and lots of stains. I know you'll want to get our scotch guard treatment. With the scotch guard, stains will lift easier and you'll extend the life of your carpet*." Though this "Golden Question©" wasn't presented in question format, it still met all of the criteria. And you guessed it, I also bought the scotch guard treatment– at an additional cost of $15 per room.

My experience with this cleaning service illustrates the power of the Golden Question©. By offering "extra value-added services" to me, the company made two additional sales. Multiply theses added sales times the number of customers they serve each day, each year, and you start to see how the "Golden Question©" can pay off.

The Golden Question© and Customer Complaints

The way we handle complaints can be one of our best opportunities to show customers how much we value their business, and it can be an opportunity to generate additional business!

The Polaroid Corporation found that when complaining customers felt completely satisfied with the resolution, they were ideal candidates for additional sales. If, for example, a customer called to complain about a problem with a camera and received an immediate solution, they could be sold additional photographic equipment on the same call.

The reason Polaroid has found success in selling additional products to customers who called to voice a complaint is because of what Janelle Barlow, author of *A Complaint Is A Gift*, calls the principle of reciprocity. The principle of reciprocity says, "*Scratch my back and I'll scratch yours*." Customers who complain and have their problems immediately resolved actually feel as though the company has done them a favor. (Of course, quickly resolving problems to the customer's satisfaction is not a favor; it's your job.) If the customer complains and receives satisfactory resolution, they are more likely to give you more business because they feel like they *owe* you.

With the case of a customer who you are engaging that has brought a complaint to your attention, craft an appropriate series and chronology of questions that could be presented that could lead to an additional sale. After you have resolved the complaint to the customer's satisfaction using the Golden Rules (Chapter Eight) and you're certain you have restored the customer's confidence in your company, employ the "Golden Question©" and ask for more business.

When I worked in car rental and a customer called to complain about a long wait in line, we'd quickly resolve the complaint using the Golden Rules (Chapter Eight) and then we asked for more business. Once we were certain that we had resolved the problem and regained the customer's goodwill, we'd say something like, "*We have an express rental program for busy travelers like you. With our express rental program there is no line wait and no paper work...you're in your car within a few minutes with no hassle.*" Very often wc were successful in enrolling customers into the express rental program **immediately** after resolving the complaint.

I believe every complaint situation is also a sales opportunity. Of course, it goes without saying that the complaining customer must be completely satisfied with the resolution before any sales attempt is made. Even in situations where you don't feel it's appropriate to offer additional products or service, you should always make every attempt to sell the company back to the customer who voiced a complaint. That is, you should work to restore the customer's confidence and completely regain their goodwill.

Complaining customers are at high risk for defection and it takes a sales effort to restore their confidence and regain their goodwill. Always end your complaint resolution process with a "Golden Question©" that reveals whether or not you have been successful in retaining the customer. An example of such a "Golden Question©" would be, *"Have we resolved this problem to your satisfaction and completely regained your goodwill?"* If the answer is no, you have some "selling" to do.

Minimizing Complaints Using the Golden Question©

Studies have found that only one person in fifty who encounters a problem will write a letter of complaint. After reading chapter eight, you know the bottom line value of customer complaints and you will, no doubt, want to capture all feedback from unhappy customers. But if only one person in 50 will tell you about a problem, how can you turn a dissatisfied customer into a loyal customer? Answer: Use the "Golden Question©" to encourage feedback and take that opportunity to restore the customer's confidence in the company and maintain their loyalty. In order to gain the opportunity to turn a complaint situation into a sales opportunity, you have to first learn about the complaint.

Several years ago I worked with a company that had a policy that all members of management must spend 25 percent of their time visiting with customers to ensure their satisfaction. Managers made a regular practice of walking up to customers asking them about their satisfaction with the service they received. Most customers reported being satisfied with the service, but some voiced complaints. When a manager received a complaint, his or her job was to do whatever it took to have the customer walk away completely satisfied. The simple "Golden Question©" technique after the sale resulted in a measurable decrease in complaints voiced to the company's headquarters and it increased customer satisfaction and most importantly, loyalty.

Discovering additional sales opportunities using the "Golden Question©" positions you to grow your business by selling more and more to your current customers. In every service situation, there is a sales opportunity. In every complaint situation there is a sales opportunity. Mine these opportunities using the "Golden Question©" and you'll realize exponential growth through additional sales from your existing customers.

Other Golden Question© Intervention Tactics

Engaging customers when they are displeased with you for a constructive outcome can be attained by deploying instant intervention tactics like:

1. **Demand an Alternative**—This technique requires you to calmly step to the side of the space (area) that you occupied at the precise time a customer engages you. Continue to let them vent while you have stepped to the side. Once they have completed their presentation of their complaint, gently point to the space you previously occupied (thus not pointing nor gesturing at them) and respectfully inquire, "What would you like us to do?" Or, "What do you feel would be a fair way to address this matter?"

2. **Let Them Vent 100 Percent**—This technique suggests that interrupting the customer in the process of venting may only serve to irritate the customer more. Have a note pad accessible so as they begin to vent, you can capture in a sincere manner the core subject matter (minus the emotion).

When they do finish, you can maintain control of your emotions and respond to the core subject matter. In many instances, the customer will calm themselves down as they see your attempt to genuinely engage them and focus upon the core subject matter being presented.

3. **Enroll Them**—Assume their participation as an advocate and involve them in solutions as if they were the hero for raising the concern to your attention.

4. **Get Their Name and Contact Information**—Immediately solicit the correct spelling of their name and a way (address, phone, email, and fax – all if possible) to follow up with them. Indicate that while you are committed to addressing the immediate concern, they have brought to your attention, you also commit to following up with them at a specific future date/time to ensure whatever solution is applied is acceptable after the fact – when emotions have subsided and logic is all present.

5. **Just Do Something**—Find something within your realm of responsibility and ability to address what the customer has brought to your attention. This will gain you constructive interaction time to then address the remainder of the concerns brought before you and time to engage your colleagues to assist with the areas outside your realm of authority.

Your ability to engage a customer, whatever their state of mind, will demand the best Service-Leader finesse on your behalf. In doing so, the BEYOND W.O.W.® affect will be experienced by both you and the customer.

PART FOUR: Building Lasting Relationships

Chapter Thirteen - *Using the "Relationship Cube©" as a Four-Step Model for Building Lasting Relationships*

Have you ever wondered what really makes a relationship with another person work? How about what it takes to cultivate and maintain healthy relationships with those that one works with (internal customers) and those who come to us (external customers)?

Well, the reverse may be easier to answer. And from that new understanding, a "Service-Leader" can begin to build the framework around which people can come together to work more effectively and connect with one another more constructively and do so in a motivated manner.

"As one of the youngest Certified Management Consultants (CMC) today, in working with organizations internationally, I have found that there are two surefire ways for individuals to self-destruct and, thereby, erode the potential of healthy customer service working relationships from ever developing." (Magee)

Organizational psychologists have found that there are commonalities with personal therapists and their research/findings with couples, as to the most prevalent reasons for this dysfunctionality—most typically manifested as conflicts and confrontations.

People tend to have conflict with one another or have difficulty connecting with others for two primary reasons:

1. *The individuals involved in a conflict are so similar* that they don't see the difficulty in the other person as being precisely what they are exhibiting themselves; or

2. That the individuals involved in the conflict or having a difficult time creating a healthy working relationship with one another may be because the *individuals involved really don't know and, thus, understand one another.*

To develop healthy relationships in the workplace as a "Service-Leader" that feed collaboration, unity, energy and motivation, consider the four basic sides to what we have found to be essential ingredients for a successful relationship—at home and in business. To build healthy relationships, concentrate as a "Service-Leader" and ask, "What are the differing 'acts/behaviors' that one can exhibit or engage in that create, reinforce or foster the four sides."

Consider motivated customer interactions and relationships as an imaginary '***Relationship Cube©***" (as first presented in ***YIELD MANAGEMENT: The Leadership Alternative To Performance and Net Profit Improvement***, by CRC Press/St. Lucie Press. ISBN# 1-57444-206-6 / USA $39.95, www.JeffreyMagee.com/library.asp) and each side is critical to holding a healthy relationship together. Visualize a cube with four labeled sides:

These 'acts/behaviors' exhibited by the "Service-Leader" in relation to each side of this "***Relationship Cube***" either reinforce constructive, lasting, loyal customer-organization standings with one another or serve as a guide to where the erosion began and how it destructed.

These four foundational sides to business relationships can either be reinforced or eroded by the very 'acts/behaviors' that you demonstrate. Consider these acts as a checklist with your customers that you have now. Which ones do you exhibit?

1. ***TRUST***—Being an example of *"honesty"* among others. People today are born with an innate 'BS' meter and can detect untruths, deception, a customer service provider who only has their own self interest in mind and will recall for eternity betrayal! Do you do what you say you will do? Do you maintain confidences of others? Are you knowledgeable of what you speak? Are you reliable?

2. ***ASSERTIVENESS***—Allow for everyone to share their *"opinions"* as long as they are even remotely close to the issues and subjects at hand. To shut down peoples' 'opinions' is almost an assured way of killing off civil interaction and discourse and an open door for aggressive behavior. Do you ask for advice and in-put from others? Do you offer to assist others without or before being asked? Do you treat others fairly? Are you flexible in the presence of others?

3. ***MOTIVATION***—Dispense a genuine, sincere *"Thank You"* to others and serve to collaboratively aid them in attaining greatness and success. When you hold them back from these destinations, the

customer may feel threatened and, thus, fight back or become passive-aggressive in their behavior towards either you or your organization. Do you respond to others in a timely manner?

4. ***COMMUNICATION***—People will sense if you are being *"open, fair and consistent"* in your pursuit of sending and receiving communication signals with all those around you. Or, if you have already concluded your position prior to them being allowed to make their case, do you listen? Do you take time to dialogue with others, or are you continually rushed? Do you interrupt others? Do you finish others sentences? Do you invite healthy dialogue among others and in groups? Do you maintain regular contact with key people internally and externally to what you do?

The act of cultivating motivated relationships with others is essential to sustained business growth, basic profitability, success and efficiency within an organization.

Customer Loyalty Begins with *Employee* Loyalty: Tips for Managers

Fundamentally, if you want to build loyal relationships with your customers, build loyal relationships with your employees. Long-term employees, naturally, have developed important product and service knowledge, which enables them to serve customers better and faster. They are more likely to take the initiative to solve problems for customers and find creative solutions to customer service challenges.

There's also proven profitability in holding on to employees. The arduous task of recruiting, screening and training is extremely costly, with many companies averaging $20,000 to $50,000 to replace just one employee. Frederick Reichheld, author of *The Loyalty Effect*, found that a 5% increase in employee retention could yield profit increases of 25% or more.

"The more chaotic the environment, the greater the need for loyalty," says Reichheld. Smart companies are finding ways to win the hearts of their employees to cut the high cost of recruiting and training new hires.

Building loyal relationships with employees makes good business sense and must be viewed as an integral part of any customer loyalty focus. When companies build loyal relationships with employees, they are preserving priceless proprietary knowledge and unique experiences and are drastically cutting recruiting and training costs. The savings resulting from retaining more employees can be invested in process improvements and solutions to better serve customers, creating even more value for your customers.

When relationships are either under attack or void of presence, this lack of healthy motivated relationships will result in a business giving customers ample reason to look elsewhere for their needs to be fulfilled. This will then be seen on the surface in declining financial numbers, a reduction in labor within an organization and lowering of moral. And this then raises its cyclical head with worsening customer interactions and a void of "Service-Leaders" rising to the occasion.

In fact, Marcus Buckingham, a Global Practice Leader with the Gallup Organization, spent the past decade surveying more than 2.5 million employees to determine key factor determinates in, "How engaged an employee will become in an organization and what causes that involvement."

Of the survey questions, three critical factors surfaced from the employee's perspective that impact customer contact performance and whether a W.O.W.® factor will ever be attained:

1. Do I know what is expected of me at work?

2. Do I have an opportunity to do what I do best every day?

3. Does my supervisor or someone at work care about me when I do excel, especially when the external customer is the beneficiary?

A "Service-Leader's" ability to foster and promote healthy relations with individuals (internal customers and external customers) will feed constructive response to these three questions.

In fact when there is the existence of a solid ***"Relationship Cube©"*** individuals will become engaged in an organization and overall passions, motivation, ownership and commitment will surface for an overall motivated group!

Chapter Fourteen - *Tapping Into Customer Mindsets for Performance Improvement Via Instant Power Surveys*

Providing a product or service to consumers because that is what you believe they want and doing so because you know that is what they want, are two different performances. One leads to profitability and sustained success performance, while the other leads to a slow death.

One of the most powerful ways to consistently ensure that you deliver the highest standard of excellence and maintain a pulse on your customer and their market place is to survey. Whether your organization undertakes the initiatives of surveying the customer base or you as an individual "Service-Leader" undertake this endeavor, there are some mechanics to rapid survey gathering that can serve you invaluably.

To effectively survey, without creating more work, first recognize that when it comes to surveying customers, you want to distinguish between two universes of customers.

You may determine to survey all of your customers. If so, make sure you code your survey instruments or collected data in such a way that you can differentiate between the two universes. Making adjustments in your Unique Selling or Service Features solely based upon the wrong universe of customer feedback can be devastating—remember the Coke-Cola debacle of the 1980's, when a change in the original flavor formula created a stir among loyal customers?

There are two distinct universes of customers, for the purpose of data solicitation and valid data collection in business surveying:

1. **Vital Few**—The core customers to your organization; the critical or essential customers that, if lost, would have a profound impact on what you do and how you operate.

2. **Useful Many**—Are all other possible customers, existing or prospective. While a business can benefit and grow with their participation, if they are lost or not matriculated, it will have no profound impact or influence on your core business and business plans.

As a "Service-Leader," whether you engage a Vital Few on the telephone, via email dialogue, face-to-face contact or are interacting via correspondence, you can determine if and when it would be appropriate to deploy a survey or merely a survey question.

In administering a survey, start first with an objective in mind. Are you seeking to gather information to:

1. Verify an action.
2. Verify a new initiative or product/service roll out.
3. Verify service standards.
4. Verify your belief systems in what you do.
5. Determine how they measure your performance in any specific area.
6. Determine how they measure the products/services that your organization provides to them, that you had no responsibility.
7. Determine if you want to gather information on what customers perceive you do best.

8. Determine if you want to gather information on what customers would like you to start offering.
9. Determine if you want to gather information on what customers perceive as your short comings.
10. Determine if you want to gather information on what customers like about possible competitors.
11. Or what?

In building your survey center base it on only three core questions:

1. **Like**—Always ask questions to solicit feedback on what customers appreciate and like about doing business with you. These are critical questions, as they reveal why they are presently exchanging their money for your goods. What they respond with should be the basis to all that you do, all product extensions and introductions and should be strongly referenced before eliminating.

   i.e. "What is the one thing you like most about doing business with us?"

2. **Add**—Always ask questions to solicit feedback on what customers would like from you that they are not receiving from you at the present time. These are critical questions, as they reveal where a customer may be taking their business outside of yours, who your competition may be, who is strategically moving in on your accounts, opportunities for additional client activity and further account connections. This feedback may also reveal, at times, what a customer seeks, that you may provide, yet they did not realize this. Thus, lost business will be revealed to you through this survey question, and the results may be very

insightful for contact purposes with both them and all other clients.

i.e. "If we were to add one new item to our portfolio that would benefit you greatest, what would you suggest we bring to market?"

3. **Stop**—Always ask questions to solicit feedback on what customers are frustrated or bothered by. In essence, the areas that they wish you could or would stop. As the continuation of this may raise their frustration to such a level that they may actually entertain options of where else to take their business.

   i.e. "What is the one thing that we do that we should stop doing—it is the least flattering aspect of our firm to you?"

Possible recipients of your survey may be: Emerging customers, prospective customers, different targeted audiences outside of traditional buyers, customers to your competition, existing customers that would otherwise be ignored, inactive (past, dead, exited) customers.

In building an actual survey instrument, you can make this exceedingly scientific or very simple and straightforward. Remember, the objective of the survey will dictate how involved you need to make it. The actual functionality of the survey (whether an electronic instrument, written instrument or gathered auditory) should be designed for fast feedback capability. Consider:

1. **Check Off**—Surveys where the responder can merely check off an answer to a prompt get the highest response rate.

2. **Fill In the Blank**—Surveys where a question is posed and requires a response that is completed in a small space area receives the second most responses, typically.

3. **Q&A**—Surveys that pose a question and ask of the responder to complete a long descriptive response receive the lowest response rate, typically.

4. **Categorize**—Build your survey if a volume of data is necessary into sections. Ideally, three sections with headers and then under that a series of related questions with a psychological chronology to them increases survey responder's comprehension and participation.

5. **Return Mechanism**—Studies indicate that whether the data can be bounced back electronically, faxed, mailed in an envelope or dropped in the mail as a response card, each gender (male and female) will respond dramatically different. Men will respond if the message is appropriate in any manner offered – it does not matter. For women, the more private the response rate (i.e. envelope devise) the greater the response percentage.

By continually surveying your customers, you can differentiate between *high-maintenance* and *high-profitability* customers. From this revelation, you can then explore, through surveying, how to better serve the high-profitability customers and grow your net bottom line!

Internal Surveys can add another level of Service-Leadership© effectiveness to your overall image.

The best feedback you can get to improve your product or service will come from customers. However, employees are also great resources for product, service, and process improvement. Consider having your employees play the role of customer for a day and also participate in problem solving meetings.

Be Your Own Customer for a Day!

A creative and very effective survey method that can lead to significant service process improvement is to be your own customer for a day. Years ago, when I worked in Consumer Affairs I found myself on the phone with a very disgruntled customer who experienced a problem with our company's product. On top of that, he had great difficulty getting answers from our Customer Care Department when he called to complain about the problem. His first words to me were, "*Have you ever called your company to experience what your customers go through*?"

Good question. Tough answer!

The bitter truth was I didn't know exactly what my customers went through when they called to voice a complaint. Certainly, I knew the logistics of complaint handling in our department, and I knew how the processes were "suppose" to work, but what was the reality? So I went on an expedition to find out exactly what my dissatisfied customers experienced when they called the Customer Care Department. I took the lesson my disgruntled customer taught me, and now I, Service Leader, experienced exactly what it's like to be their own customer. I challenge **you** to be your own customer for a day within the next 30 days. In *Customer Satisfaction Is Worthless. Customer Loyalty Is Priceless*, Jeffrey Gitomer presents a simple menu for a revealing "*be your own customer for a day*" experience. Do one, some or all of the following (based loosely on Gitomer's survey) to get a real feel for customer service in your organization.

1. **Call 30 minutes before your phone lines are turned on.** Is your recording friendly, informative? What would you want to hear if you had an emergency after hours?
2. **Call at exactly 5:00pm.** Was the phone answered? Were your questions answered fully, just as if it were 10:00 a.m.?
3. **Call up ballistic** – Be demanding and irate. Does it end good or bad?
4. **Call during lunch or any peak period.** How long do you hold?
5. **Ask for the president**. Does your employee work to find out how they might help you and make you feel good about the encounter even when they don't transfer you? Or do they transfer you?
6. **Visit your website**. How customer-friendly is it? How accurate is the information on the site? Does it take too many clicks to get help? Does information seem to be hidden"? Is the site *useful* to customers?
7. **Send a complaint letter**. How long does it take to get a response? Is the response one that would restore your confidence and regain your goodwill? Would you remain a customer of *your* company?
8. **Send a complaint email**. How quick and satisfactory is the response?
9. **Spend a day using your product or service**. Was the service experience something you'd rave about? If not, why not?

Conducting this simple "customer for a day" survey may leave you surprised or disappointed. The good news is you'll know what your customers go through and better understand their expectations. The next step is to **change everything that you find unacceptable.**

Hold Problem Solving Meetings

Put together a diverse team within your company and meet regularly to discuss top problems and customer concerns. The objective of the meetings is to identify the root-cause of customer impacting problems and eliminate those problems at the root. The team can include people from Sales & Marketing, the frontline, Information Technology, and even Accounting. The idea is to view the problems from many different perspectives and to explore preventative steps that will be executed smoothly and effectively. You might consider setting some ground rules for the meetings such as: no one (department) is allowed to offer excuses or alibis for customer impacting problem or if it's a problem for the customer, it's a problem that needs to be explored. The meetings should be structured and highly focused using systematic problem solving approaches. When problem solving meetings are held regularly and run effectively, they become an incredible resource for organizations by continually monitoring problems, identifying root-causes, and eliminating problems at the root.

Being your own customer for a day and holding regular problem solving meetings will lead to great insight on customer expectations and current problems, and these practices will position you to improve the overall customer service experience.

The number of businesses, customer contact professionals and bosses that administer a survey regularly or ever, is surprisingly low!

To accentuate your relevance as a service provider and bring out the Service-Leader within you, one must create a climate whereby one feels compelled, intrinsically, to regularly survey, whether through visual instruments, auditory exchanges or kinesthetic interactions. The "Service-Leader" attains a BEYOND W.O.W.© standing by continuously connecting with these "Vital Few" and scrutinizing the data that comes in from the marketplace.

The hidden success factor is in inviting customers into a role of ownership by involving them in the feedback loop to:

1. Provide solutions to problems that they have experienced from their outside perspective and ways to address them, without the benefit or detriment of being prejudiced to industry information as you are;

2. Suggest new offerings that may have been outside your thinking circle; and

3. Assist in crises resolution.

A classic example of an industry struck by the scarcity mentality and operating from a daily business model of fear and short sightedness would be the travel industry. Whether it is placing blame on the terrorist events of September 11, 2001, the bursting out of control economy of the 1990s, the Gulf War, SARS in international travel circles or whatever, it is amazing how an industry was profitable on September 10, 2001, and then in one day, they raked up billion dollar deficits?

A great example of an industry that has done nothing, detailed in this book, to this Chapter and an industry that if any one player were to draw upon these proven power points could create a legacy envied by others.

Not a single survey to their most loyal (Vital Few) customers. Not a single survey inviting suggestions, input, business coast saving examples or ways to regain market share and profitability.

In one great example after September 11, a letter was sent to Continental Airlines detailing a need for 30 round trip non-stop flights in 2002 on their airlines. An estimated $46,000 in ticket purchases guaranteed at a time when the airlines was announcing more than ten thousand lay offs, in exchange for a matching frequent flyer status to their direct competitor, with the ability of these non-stop flights. Amazingly, a letter came back from their Director of Customer Loyalty saying "NO WAY."

That, in fact, is a powerful W.O.W.® factor and not the intended BEYOND WOW from a positive perspective, it is, although, a wickedly outrageous what factor! After a short communication exchange, it became obvious that the business was not desired. One week later the CEO of Continental announced the lay off of thousands of additional employees – the Director of Loyalty Marketing was not one of them.

A final letter was sent explaining a way that Continental could significantly increase market share, revenue and profitability, while at the same time winning proven "Vital Few" customers from other airlines to them, again, "NOT INTERESTED," WOW!

I guess even when I try to give a competitor money, business, traffic I am forced to remain loyal to their competition and my previous travel partner—I WILL FLY AMERICAN! (See Chapter twenty).

Chapter Fifteen - *Ensuring Your Survivability by Planting New "Target Rich Environments" (TRE's©)*

The forgotten "Target Rich Environment" (TRE©) that you can mine for golden opportunities and lasting account relationships, are overlooked by most customer service providers and organizational leaders alike. Don't miss the greatness that lies directly within your reach.

Business professionals have long since been introduced to the Italian economist and land owner Pareto's observation of 100 years past, that 80 percent of the Italian land and wealth being held by less than 20 percent of the population. From this observation has come the parallel that 80 percent of business transactions typically take place with 20 percent of one's client base—hence the "80/20 Rule."

In exploring ways to cultivate greater levels of customer contact, business transactions and overall increased productivity, and more importantly, profitability from one's activities, a "Service-Leader" must re-acclimate their behavior and those of the professionals around them to recognize how to be cutting edge in all that they do.

There are two powerful ways to provide a higher level of customer care, increase market share and cultivate lasting relationships with customers at the same time. Consider:

FIRST - The "Ruck-Magee Curve©" is the "New 80/20 Rule" and as a customer service business building model or selling effectiveness model can best be explained by visualizing or drawing a bell curve. Label both ends of the curve with a 10 percent factor and the middle with an 80 percent factor. The new 80/20 Rule (a.k.a., "The Ruck-Magee Curve©" as detailed within, ***THE SALES TRAINING HANDBOOK: 52 Quick, Easy To Lead Mini Seminars***, by Magee and published by McGraw-Hill Publishers, ISBN# 0-07-137516-3), indicates that within any buying market, that market will always break down into three subsets – 80/10/10 or the "New 80/20 Rule."

There will always be 10 percent of a market that will never be customers (negative to your cause, pro someone else, have no need for your offer, etc.) and a 10 percent that will always be a customer (positive to your cause, pro you—an advocate, has need for your exact offer, etc.). Most customer service and even traditional selling professionals (those tasked with bringing in more business accounts for an organization or cultivating additional levels of business from existing accounts) and organizational leaders tend to focus a disproportionate amount of time, energy and resources to grow that competitive 10 percent already identified to be a suitable prospect or customer.

Most often that time is actually incorrectly applied to that identified "Target Rich Environment!"

While it is critical to first ensure all efforts are applied smartly to this 10 percent, you should also assign activities toward that 80 percent in the middle of the curve that are potentially buyers of your product, that may appear neutral to a cause at the outset, or don't know that you offer said services/products, etc. If properly engaged and given a reason to do so would become active clients, as well. It is this 80 percent that most all organizations and individuals miss in their customer service development and account selling strategies.

That 80 percent is a true growth market. There may even be 80 percent within your present customer line up, recognizable as those accounts that you would traditionally overlook and assume to be not a good fit for other products and services you offer. Yet, you have actually never really pursued a dialogue with your customer to determine if there is, in fact, an opportunity with them or within the overall organization they represent and which they could network you towards.

Look at parallel markets to where you are active presently—where you're 10 percent engaged now. Look at the partnerships, affiliations, institutional connections, individual referrals and advocates you presently have within your 10 percent portion of that "Ruck-Magee Curve." Now evaluate where similar contacts can be cultivated from within that 80 percent market.

And the power of this 80 percent is that most customer service nor sales professionals, call on them—there is no active relationship!

Organizations typically think of increased market growth or increased market share by falling back on product line extensions, new products introductions to existing market contacts or bundling products together in different ways. Still most of the efforts are targeted toward that same 10 percent of the market that people have become comfortable with as buyers—quick wins.

SECOND – The concept of the "Target Rich Environment" (TRE) applied to the "Ruck-Magee Curve" may also be applied to every existing account you call upon to identify additional "Target Rich Environments," both horizontally to your present customer contact (as identified as an individual and business unit), as well as vertically (identified as how deep can you establish contacts and possible additional customers).

There are countless applications of this model. One application would be simply to apply this model and weigh your daily customer service activities against it by drawing a tree (tree equals TRE) on a piece of paper. Within the foliage portion of the top of the tree, label it with your dominant customer type, meaning universal industry name. Now draw branches outward from the trunk of your tree and across each branch label it with only the specific type of customers that you "presently" have under that category (names of actual organizations that are buyers of your product or service).

Add only the appropriate number of branches for the "present" active customers you have. Once you have this completed, brainstorm (partner with another colleague or advocate, if necessary or possible), identify all ***other*** possible additional branches that could be added for that tree (TRE) that you are not actively serving.

Typically, what you will find is that the contacts on your primary tree (TRE) are only a limited number of opportunity points. You can grow your primary TREE by expanding into all of the points of contact available for your best client contact—hence your primary 10 percent will be more actively engaged and cultivated. Studies also indicate a customer buying pattern in the organizations where a vendor and buyer have deep and rich relationships with multiple entry contacts points to one another's organizations, multiple buyers or multiple products and services, the greater that relationship becomes. The greater the relationship the more inclined one another is to work with in good and difficult times!

Another application of the "Target Rich Environment" concept can be further applied, once this primary drill is thoroughly developed. Draw additional trees on separate sheets of paper, then identify possible customers to every product or service line, independent of pre-existing mindsets and historical business patterns. By recognizing the offer that you are not presently engaging others on and which others may not be engaging as well, you will identify great customer service opportunities for growing your business—hence the 80 percent market of the "Ruck-Magee Curve."

With each parallel TRE identified, now drill down that tree and identify all of the possible branches where you can come into contact with them for prospect-to-customer conversion.

The forgotten "Target Rich Environment" that you can mine for golden opportunities and lasting account relationships, which most customer service, sales and management professionals miss, could, in fact, impact an organization's greatness. It lies directly within their reach.

Two action plans for increased customer service client development opportunities are:

1. Apply the "Ruck-Magee Curve" to determine if you are thoroughly taking care of and developing your existing 10 percent market share factor.

2. Ask the question with the aid of the "TRE" model how best to address the overlooked 80 percent market share factor.

Significant business awaits the smart "Service-Leader" professional in a market today. There has never been a better time to take care and connect with your customer…now is the time for the deployment of the "Reliable CARE" model.

Imagine you grow apples (your product/service) as your business in an apple orchard (your market), and that is all you do. This year a bug comes through your orchard (market) that only eats apples, what is the net outcome to your business?

To remain balanced and wealthy, you should be continuously planting and grooming other trees (TRE) into your orchard (market).

And, if you did have this orchard, you would find yourself routinely feeding your trees, cultivating each tree independent of the others, and you would continuously be pruning back over growth (detractors to what you should be doing), cleaning out dead limbs (branches representing each buyer) and further nurturing the ones remaining visible.

Most individuals plant their trees and then look for the low hanging fruit to harvest (business transactions, sales, etc). In the past few years, all of the low hanging fruit has been taken and more orchards have appeared in the market. As long as you only look at the low hanging fruit (the traditional branches that you identify and work), you will continue to miss the abundant opportunities possible in every orchard due to not looking upward further into the tree (TRE) for new emerging opportunities (branches) nor will you grow new opportunities (new branches of other advocates, influencers, gate keepers, individuals to whom you know and who become promoted in the future as new buyers, etc.).

The remaining question in route to BEYOND W.O.W.® experiences and greater tree opportunities, is how many trees you have and how many branches you can climb in route to the top of your orchard?

Every business today can be doing immediately better, if individuals would stop stressing over the lack of low hanging opportunities and look upward for greater opportunities and continually plant new trees and groom stronger branches in every act they engage in.

Chapter Sixteen - *The Loyalty Advantage The Proven Path to Growth and Increased Profits*

Business is about winning customers and keeping customers. A lot of companies do a great job of winning customers. In fact, many companies have realized exponential growth solely through their acquisition strategy. But too many companies, far too many companies, fail to put processes in place to keep the customers they've worked so hard to win. And this is a problem because business growth is stunted when companies don't combine a focused retention strategy with acquisition efforts. Business growth is obtained by doing one of two things:

1. Gaining market share
2. Gaining customer share

Most organizations today have as part of their strategic goal, a strategy to increase market share. To achieve growth through gaining market share is to sell to more and more customers. Organizations do this through aggressive sales and marketing campaigns, mergers and acquisitions, and product expansions. But there is another path to growth and profit increase that many companies either fail to realize is available to them, or they fail to mobilize efforts to make it happen for them, and that is to grow by gaining "customer share."

To achieve growth through gaining "customer share" is to provide a higher level of meaningful customer service and sell more and more to your current customers. You sell more and more to your current customers by getting them to stay with you, spend more with you, and recommend you (often) to people in their network.

The sole purpose of this chapter is to help you keep your best customers coming back again and again, get them to spend more and more on your products and services, and tell their friends (thus becoming an advocate for you) about your company and what you offer.

The proven profitability of loyalty is experienced when you increase your "customer share." You make your customers more profitable, and hence, you add net profit to the bottom line.

Increase your retention by 5% and increase your profitability by 85 percent!

Frederick Riechheld, in the New York Times Best Seller, *The Loyalty Effect*, discusses findings that when a company increases their customer retention rate by a mere 5%, the average return on investment is between 25% and 85%. This profit increase may sound dramatic, but it's concrete and measurable. Studies indicate that it costs five times more to win a customer than it does to keep a current customer. Here are four more reasons gains in customer share result in bottom line increase (as summarized in *The Loyalty Effect* by Frederick Riechheld):

1. **Loyal customers are the easiest customers to serve**—Over time, you learn the preferences of customers, and they become more educated on the scope of your offerings. This knowledge of expectations on both ends leads to decreased transaction

time and fewer problems, which saves you money.

2. **Long-term customers tend to spend more with you than new customers**—In a loyalty study of more than 100 companies, an auto-service company found that the expected profit of a fourth year customer is more than triple that of a first year customer. As the business-to-customer relationship grows, profits increase.

3. **Happy, loyal customers purchase other products or services in the company's line**—Resulting, again, in increased profits.

4. **Satisfied, loyal customers recommend the company's products or services**—A recommendation from a friend or colleague can be a decisive influence on purchasing choices.

Generally, increasing your customer retention rate by just 5% can lead to a profit increase of up to 85%.

When companies combine a focused acquisition strategy with a fierce retention strategy, then growth, profit increase, and lasting value is the inevitable result.

Building "customer share" is customer loyalty. If you want to grow your business exponentially, you must get serious about building and maintaining loyal relationships with your customers (and acknowledge that an acquisition strategy alone will not guarantee growth).

There are four specific steps you must take to build a customer retention strategy so you can increase the bottom line with significant leaps in customer share.

1. Turn first-time buyers into repeat customers.
2. Forget customer satisfaction, strive for customer loyalty.
3. Launch loyalty-marketing campaigns.
4. Focus on getting 100% of the business from 100% of your customers.

1. Turning first-time buyers into repeat customers: The first step toward building a profitable base of loyal customers is to get the first-time buyer to come back. Turning first-time buyers into repeat customers is achieved by getting to know your customers, creating superior value, and building relationships with your customers.

Know Your Customers. The more you know about your customers, the better you can serve and sell to them—and the better positioned you are to keep them. You cannot build relationships with customers you don't know. Companies come to know their customers by collecting data about customers and using that data to proactively anticipate customer needs and exceed their expectations. In an interview with USA Today, Phil Satre, CEO of Harrah's, discussed the company's loyalty program, which is driven by their ability to capture critical information about customers:

Suppose we sign up a new customer in Atlantic City. He lives hundreds of miles from the casino and plays $50 in a nickel slot machine over two hours. We know that person is a casual gambler who just happens to be in Atlantic City.

However, if he lives in (nearby) Philadelphia and plays $500 on a sophisticated slot machine, our predictive model says he is a lucrative customer, who probably wandered in from the competition. Within a week, we have a thank-you to his home and an offer customized by our technology and expertise to bring him back.

So how does a company get valuable customer information? At Harrah's, here's how it works:

We have them fill out enrollment forms by offering them rewards. Then we give them a card that tracks their play. We require basic information such as phone numbers and e-mail addresses. If they want, they can give us more information, such as if they like Italian food.

The more you know about your customers, the better positioned you are to deliver customized service to bring them back.

Create Superior Value. "Customers today are strongly value oriented." This statement appeared in a recent article in the Harvard Business Review. The authors explain that value to customers is the results they receive in relation to the total costs (both the price and the other costs to customers incurred in acquiring the service). In other words, **customers want a fair return on investment when they do business with you**. To create value for your customers, make sure you deliver the level of service they expect and deserve and work hard to deliver more than they expect.

One of my clients, The Scotts Company, has found a way to create superior value for customers, while at the same time building and strengthening loyalty. When customers register online for the Scotts Lawn Care or Gardening Reminder Service, Scotts contacts them periodically by e-mail to tell them just what to do — and when — to help customers maintain a healthy lawn and beautiful gardens. In addition, they send special e-mail alerts with recommendations when their consultants note a particular problem developing in the customer's area, such as drought or a problem pest. The service is free, keeps the company and its brands top of mind, and you bet it generates and maintains loyalty. (I know, because not only is Scotts my client, I am their LOYAL customer!)

Build Relationships. *"If you don't make an emotional connection with customers, then satisfaction is worthless."* William J. McEwen and John H. Fleming

If your goal is to get your customers coming back again and again, they have to feel like they are more than an account number…they have to have a relationship with you. Tim Sanders, Chief Solutions Officer at Yahoo talks about the impacting difference between serving customers and building relationships with customers in his book, Love is the Killer App:

> *Think of the difference between the relationship you have with a self-service gas station and your dry cleaner. You don't know a soul at the gas station and you'll stop at a different one when it's more convenient or offers a better price. But if you have a good, consistent relationship with your dry cleaner, they can raise their prices or you can move six blocks; you'll remain a patron because of your history. So even when my cleaners once lost a shirt—something that might normally send me into a fit—I forgave them because I liked them and because I trusted that they would eventually atone (which they did a few months later when I needed a suit cleaned and pressed in less than an hour; they did it happily).*

When you have relationships with customers, they are more forgiving, more loyal, and in general, feel more satisfied.

Capture important information about your customers beginning with their first transaction, constantly create value and make relationship building your goal, and you will quickly turn first-time buyers into repeat customers!

2. Forget Satisfaction, Strive for Loyalty. Four reasons to be a fierce customer loyalty advocate, and not focus on customer satisfaction:

ONE - Customer satisfaction means NOTHING these days. The truth is, today's customers expect mediocre service. Apathy is expected. Late is expected. Problems are expected. No follow-through is expected. As long as companies don't go below these **very low** expectations, customers are satisfied.

TWO - Customer satisfaction = "Sufficient or Adequate Service." When a company achieves "customer satisfaction," what it has really achieved is getting customers to feel that the service is adequate or sufficient—that it wasn't horrible. The customer's expectations, typically very low expectations, were met. That's all customer satisfaction means.

THREE - Customers report being "satisfied" only because their expectations are so low, and no one else is doing any better.

FOUR - Satisfied customers are not your customers. They're just with you until they find something better.

Customer satisfaction is a feeling…a feeling that low expectations have been met. Customer loyalty, on the other hand, is a set of behaviors that produce revenue.

- ✍ Loyal customers by definition don't defect.
- ✍ Loyal customers reward the company by buying from you again and again.
- ✍ Loyal customers buy other products or services in your line.
- ✍ Loyal customers tell people in their network about your company (referrals). That is, they actually market for you and word-of-mouth advertising is the most persuasive form of advertising.

Does loyalty versus a feeling of satisfaction really impact profits? You bet it does! Take a look at this case study.

> One of my colleagues, Ed Peters of the *4Profit Institute*, conducted a large customer satisfaction survey that provides irrefutable proof that the difference between satisfaction and loyalty can be a "million dollar difference." Ed's survey for a men's clothing store in the Midwest found that customers who had an "excellent" shopping experience (48%) visited the stores an average of 3.9 times a year and spent an average of $465 per visit. Customers who merely had a "good" experience (49%) visited 3.5 times a year and spent only $397 per visit. Excellent service is what builds customer loyalty. Good customer service results in customer satisfaction. Now look at this…the difference between an "excellent" experience and a "good" experience was half a visit per year and $68 in sales – or about $3.2 million a year in lost sales.

As a "Service-Leader," stop striving for high customer satisfaction and focus on delivering truly "Exceptional" service (as detailed on CSI Model, see Chapter Six)—service that results in a profitable base of loyal customers. Satisfied customers will give you a "good" ranking on a survey today and leave you for the competition tomorrow. Loyal customers return again and again, recommend your company often and significantly add to your bottom line!

3. **Launch Loyalty Marketing Campaigns.** By now you are probably convinced that retaining more customers and selling more and more to your existing customers is a solid business strategy that can lead to significant growth and profit increase. Given the significant profit potential available from gaining customer share, it only makes sense that you would want to take every opportunity to strengthen relationships with customers. One way to do that is through Loyalty Marketing. Loyalty Marketing is a strategy that is all about getting more business from your best customers. Your existing customers are your best sales prospects and your best opportunity to maximize profit.

Loyalty Marketing is a strategy that is all about getting more business from your best customers.

A loyalty marketing campaign is planned and launched in the same manner as any ad campaign. The only difference between a "regular" campaign and a loyalty marketing campaign is that in loyalty marketing campaigns, you fiercely focus on staying in front of and strengthening loyalty with your best and most profitable customers. Loyalty marketing is one-to-one communication via a planned schedule of targeted messages. Here are three tips to help you design your loyalty marketing campaign.

ONE - Identify your best, most profitable customers. Every company has profitable customers, customers that cost the company money, and customers somewhere in the middle. Your target customers for loyalty marketing campaigns will be your most profitable customers. For example, when I worked in car rental, the most profitable customers were business customers who rented 20 times or more annually. These customers, though the minority, generated more profits than the larger group of leisure renters. Determine who your best customers are, calculate their net worth to your company, and design a campaign to keep them doing business with you.

TWO - Never let a customer get more than 60 days away from you. Keep in touch with your most valuable customers on a regular basis and make sure you never let 60 days pass between communications. Send notes, emails, drop by—anything to keep the communication going.

THREE - Use a variety of mediums to communicate with your best customers. Don't limit your loyalty marketing campaign to sales announcements and print media. Take clients to lunch, make personal phone calls, and invite customers to participate in focus groups. I am constantly looking for creative ways to stay in touch with my most valuable customers. We send out Valentine's Day cards every February with a brief note saying, "*We love doing business with you.*" We also send out

Thanksgiving cards, a weekly content-rich eZine, and make phone calls regularly to clients…all to stay connected with our most valued customers.

The whole idea behind loyalty marketing is for you to get more business from your best and most profitable customers…because your existing customers are your best opportunity to maximize profit.

4. Focus Upon Getting 100% from 100%. Could you be leaving money on the table? After delivering a keynote address at one of my banking client's annual meeting, I sat at the back of the auditorium and listened to the president's speech. The president was exhorting his employees to "*Get 100% of the business from 100% of our customers*." He explained that all too often, the bank settled for offering one or two services to a customer and failed to ask for more business.

> "*Take the customer who has a personal checking account with us and that is the only service we provide them. Do you think this customer has credit cards? What about a mortgage, car loan, annuity, or a CD? They may have one or all of these services…**with our competitors**. The need for the service is there. We have to identify the need and ask for the business.*"

This president is smart. The average banking customer needs much more than a personal checking account, and the possibility for service opportunities are endless. A proactive sales person will discover what the customer needs and find a way to meet those needs at her bank. Think about this

> president's words: *"Get 100% of the business from 100% of our customers.*" Are you getting 100% of the business you could possibly get from every one of your customers? Don't assume that all of the business you're currently getting is all you can get.

As you read (and re-read) this chapter, it is my sincere desire that you gain specific strategies to increase your customer share exponentially and that you walk away with the inspiration to truly make these new strategies work. Give some serious thought to what your business would look like if you kept more of the customers you won and you were able to sell 100% of your services/products to those customers? Also give serious thought to what your business will look like if you lose as many customers as you win and if you undersell to the few customers you have.

"Customer share" can be attained as a "Service-Leader" provider through these four specific steps, and when actively implemented and sustained customer retention occurs, and increase to the bottom line leaps!

Chapter Seventeen - *Customers as Allies: Cultivating, Utilizing and Maintaining Them Strategically*

Business is about winning customers and keeping customers. When you have a customer relationship where the customer comes to you, raves about you and sends others to you, you have an Ally and an Advocate.

The "Service-Leader" provider realizes that cultivating allies is actually a matter of doing what a customer service provider already does in many instances. It merely involves doing certain things in a different manner.

For one organization, they have allies and another has what it feels are continuous problems with their customers not appreciating all the extra things that they provide to them. Here is where simple actions yield significant differences.

Start by eliminating entitlement mindsets from prospective and active customers, and strive to ensure that all customers appreciate and value the relationship that you are forging.

Consider every organization has a pre-set policy of how to engage customers and what service standards are to be delivered. If a customer service provider does this, then an organization may imply that we are functioning at peak performance. This level of service transaction might be referred to as providing "Level 'A'" customer service.

Now, imagine an upset or ballistic customer comes to a service provider and is upset over what they feel is an inadequacy. Most service providers would attempt to address this, and in their pursuit, even deliver a little extra as their way of saying, "I am sorry for your troubles." Sound about right?

Well, in doing so, the service provider has not moved from delivering "Level 'A'" customer service to delivering "Level 'B'" customer service. And, if you do so without somehow qualifying that gesture, the customer most times will feel as if they were entitled to that extra. Then, the next time that customer does business with you, their expectation is set for "Level 'B'" and that is typically what they receive. With this cyclical process, many organizations have customers paying par for goods and services, yet receiving "Level 'A to Z'" customer service standards.

Ally Building Formula:
Extra=Favor/Courtesy=Qualify=Appreciation=Ally!

With this, they have very few loyal customers, advocates, and, in tough times, no allies!

To build "allies" is to build a profitable base of loyal customers, and this doesn't happen by accident. It takes a focused and rigorous plan of action. First, convert this simple customer engagement process around and consider "Three Alliance Building Action" plans. Next, develop an Alliance Building Plan based on our five proven steps for building and maintaining loyal relationships with customers:

1. **Qualify Your "Level 'B'" Actions**—Whenever you provide anything beyond "Level 'A'" customer service to any customer, always in a non-disrespectful manner, ensure that you communicate (either at the time or in a follow-up action after the

fact) that the "Level 'B'" is not a norm and may not always be doable.

By doing so, you will establish a loyalty appreciation level and that becomes from where allies grow outward from in the future. These relationships will typically evolve into customers that their loyalty will earn them "Vital Few" category status.

2. **Survey**—Continuously engage your "Vital Few'" and solicit feedback from them on their perspectives to their *"likes, adds, and stops"* and see them warm up to you, take ownership with you and defend you.

3. **Staying Connected**—Never let your best customers get more than 30 to 60 days out. Always say, "Thank You," and keep connected on more than just a business transaction basis.

Turn customers into allies using solid action plans and you'll dramatically increase customer retention and your bottom line. You can begin to cultivate greater levels of loyalty and advocates from customers by changing simple engagement behaviors demonstrated every day in every business one simple way.

Rebuilding an "Appreciative" Customer From an "Entitled," Ungrateful Customer

Another way to recognize how a business gets itself into a situation where difficult and angry customers become common place starts by recognizing how you do not create appreciative customers.

By building "Appreciative" customers, you gain repeat business and allies for life.

Imagine for a moment that how your business has pre-determined the best way to engage a customer, and thus, how to treat a customer is called "A." Now visualize a typical customer coming to you, and you have been trained to deliver "A" level of service. By doing so, the business is profitable and the customer will be happy.

Now, on one occasion you are confronted by an upset customer, now ask yourself, "What is human tendency?"

Do you treat this customer by delivering level "A," less than level "A" or do you extend something more than level "A" service?

For most professionals placed into this position, delivering more than level "A" service is the norm. Now, if this is delivered to a customer outright, the problem that is created at this elementary stage, is the customer feels they are entitled to this new level of service that we call, "B."

Then, the next time that customer returns, do they expect "A" or "B?" What do you or your colleagues typically deliver? Now, let's compound this interaction with a customer gaining level "B," and then there is a problem in the future with them. Now you find yourself doing, again, the extra (more than "A" and more than "B").

Now, you probably find yourself at level "C" service, and the creation of customers feeling and being trained to expect extra every time.

To turn this process around and create "appreciative" customers that appreciate you and what you deliver to them, consider the following five step engagement approach:

1. Always recognize that when you deliver more than "A" level of service, either recognize that the act you have just delivered is, in fact, EXTRA—more than "A."

2. In your mind and that of your business, this act of delivering more than "A" or extra service is a FAVOR (courtesy, gesture, gift) from your perspective, and if you do nothing to establish this in the customer's mind, then you run the risk that the customer sees it as entitlement.

3. So, if you do not want to grant that act of extra away, then you must always find a way to QUALIFY in your customer's mind's-eye that what you are providing is, in fact, beyond "A," and that you are pleased to be able to provide "B" at this time, and that you may not always be able to deliver this.

4. Then, do this exchange in such a way that by qualifying that act, you can solicit some degree of FEEDBACK from the customer that qualifies the act.

5. By doing so, the customer now elevates the simple act of delivering extra ("B") that you may see as a favor, as extra, and their feedback will be registered in their mind as EXTRA. Now, they will publicly APPRECIATE the "B" you have provided to them.

What is most important about this new dialogue exchange is that you have elevated your skill base to that of a Service-Leader and have now turned a typical customer interaction around and created a conduit for cultivating lasting advocates and repeat customers.

PART FIVE: Shut Up, No One Cares

Chapter Eighteen—
World Class "Crappy Service"

Chapter Nineteen—
The DNA Revisited

Chapter Eighteen - ***World Class "Crappy Service"***

Business is about winning customers and keeping customers. A lot of companies today demonstrate how best to alienate a customer and lose them!

Whether it is due to an entitlement culture created in the last generation in our service economy (review the previous Chapter on getting back to "A"), lack of people skills or people being held accountable for their actions and behavior, what is obvious is that "crappy service" is prevalent all around one today.

If you reflect upon your own customer service experiences, you too can come up with a myriad of examples at the "Crappy" end of the pendulum and the WOW end.

Here are some situations for you to reflect. Do you have similar experiences? More importantly, do you have analogies like these that your customers might point fingers towards you? What is most critical in the context of this book, as you read these or reflect upon your own recent experiences as a customer, is to consider to critical questions:

FIRST, is to recognize why the situation even arose and how it could have been avoided. SECOND, is to evaluate in your mind instant solutions to said event!

Not what BEYOND WOW® is about, would be these daily occurrences in the life of customers:

1. The airline that penalizes its most valuable passengers, most frequent flyers by now saying

free upgrades, which costs that airline a negligible amount of money. They forgot that for a passenger
2. to receive one, they would have had to have bought passage on their plane.

3. The restaurant that offers merely an apology to the business patron (a Vital Few!) who finds a live cockroach climbing out of their salad plate at dinner.

4. The rental car company who places an executive into a go-cart when they have a line up of upscale cars and a lack of business.

5. The couple at dinner late in the evening and the waiter who does not offer them free dessert from the dessert cart, as they finish the dinner, of items that will otherwise be removed from the line up at the end of the evening.

6. To the major airline that denies a most frequent of flyer with a competitor who wants to bring them tens-of-thousands of dollars of business if they will match his frequent flyer status with their competitor.

7. The limo car service that breaks down in the snow, doesn't get stuck in the snow, strands the customer, provides no alternative options and the customer takes it upon them self to hitch hike to get to their destination.

8. The store where the service rep is more interested in their social dialogue on the telephone, as opposed to the patron standing in front of them.

9. To flight attendant that would rather stand in the galley during the entire boarding process and right up through to departure ignoring the passengers and provides no "hello" or assistance while boarding, and then wonders why people have a bitter attitude towards them.

10. The dry cleaners that merely re-presses clothes without cleaning the item and then gets upset when asked to redo.

11. And the best for last…recognized across the globe for quality and perceived service would be Daimler-Chrysler and their Mercedes brand and Lexus. In a recent mystery customer experience, both scored "POOR" on the Customer Service Index® presented in this book!

    In fact the vehicles taken in for service and a routine check-up came back with grease stains throughout the vehicle and a price quote for service four-times that of the industry norm in that community (Mercedes) and with additional mechanical problems that were not present when the vehicle was initially taken in (Lexus). And when this was brought to the attention of the vendor, the low score plummeted with their cavalier attitudes.

What makes each of these above situations most alarming and humorous is that they actually occurred!

Business is about winning customers and keeping customers. A lot of companies today demonstrate how best to alienate a customer and lose them.

Chapter Nineteen - *The DNA Revisited*

Business is about winning customers and keeping core business unit customers for life.

As a "Service-Leader" the infrastructure necessary to fulfill that objective may take on the face of:

1. Attitude and the personality mettle appropriate to interface with customer type of stuff.

2. Mission Statement/MAP making stuff.

3. Understanding that customers really want one of or a combination of four types of stuff.

4. Reliable CARE actions.

5. Understanding that customer service can be a profit center type of stuff.

6. Realizing how to immediately, objectively and accurately measure your level of customer service upon a measurement index type of stuff.

7. Realizing that your leadership style impacts performance outcomes type of stuff.

8. Realizing and knowing how to deal with complaints can be good stuff.

9. Knowing how to design and deploy service recovery stuff.

10. ALWAYS knowing how to sandwich angry customers is good stuff.

11. Using golden questions can be great stuff.

12. Knowing the stuff that relationship building is made from.
13. Using surveys can be explosive stuff.

14. Cultivating your TREs© is essential stuff.

15. Knowing the stuff that loyalty is made from.

16. Having allies is bottom line good stuff.

17. Avoiding being accused of providing crappy service is good stuff.

18. Knowing how to win back a lost customer is profitable stuff.

19. Making moments always truthfully positive stuff is necessary.

20. Always growing your business involves a lot of STUFF!

As a "Service-Leader," having healthy DNA makes winning at the customer service game easier. Having unhealthy DNA may mean serious internal reviews as to whether you have the right infrastructure, personnel, skill and knowledge levels, leadership, support mechanisms in place and a desire among yourself and others to win.

It is amazing how some individuals in similar industries facing the same market trends and issues can have such radically different approaches to their job and bottom line.

DNA in the form of cultural, personnel, rewards, quality of life, labor and management relationships among many items makes this a reality.

So, do you have an organizational DNA and personal DNA that signals an entitlement mentality, which leads to implosions and minimal loyalty moments or a DNA of endowment appreciation for all that is around you?

PART Six: Winning Customers for Life

Chapter Twenty—
Winning Back the Lost Customers & Evaluating the Lifetime Value of a Customer

Chapter Twenty-One—
"Moments Of Truth" and One Percent Factors to Ensure "Service-Leadership©" Mindsets and Behaviors

Chapter Twenty-Two—
Thirty Plus W.O.W.® Ways to Grow Your Business Now

Chapter Twenty

Winning Back Lost Customers & Evaluating the Lifetime Value of a Customer

Customer win back is proactively identifying customers who have left or who are on the brink of defection and developing a strategic initiative to try to win them back. Customer win back is a powerful strategy that can lead to huge profit potential.

Studies show that companies can successfully sell back to 20% to 40% of lost customers—when they try. But most companies simply let lost customers walk.

In this chapter, you will explore real-world examples for winning back lost customers and an easy-to-implement six step plan to help you launch your own win back strategy for big profits.

I WILL NEVER FLY "Yo u Know Who" AIRLINES AGAIN!

By most people's definition, we are frequent flyers. Last year alone, we logged nearly 400 flights. Most of those flights, about 90%, were on one primary airline. Being a frequent flyer, one becomes accustomed to the many delays: weather, mechanical problems, last-minute refueling, announcements stating that the flight crew is en route from the East coast while you're sitting at an airport in the Midwest—you name it and it has happened. Several thousand miles ago, getting upset about delays disappeared and an attitude (see Chapter One) of just "deal with it" to be proactive and productive developed. That was until I was *forced* to spend 12 hours in an airport.

It was in route to D.C. for a big event, in which an electrical lighting storm erupted while coming into the airport. Consequently, the airport shut down for about 35 minutes. This short shut down threw everything into total chaos. An hour and a half later, the eight letters no traveler ever wants to see illuminated in red next to my flight number—**C A N C E L E D**.

I got booked on the next flight out which didn't leave for *another two hours.* Two and a half hours *after* that flight was scheduled to leave, it was canceled!

The next flight I got booked on also canceled. It was a full 12 hours and nine minutes *after* the initial arrival that the departure for D.C. occurred. Livid, I vowed never to fly this airline again. That is until eight days later when I got a letter in the mail from an executive with that airline. The letter read:

> *Our manager in Dallas/Ft. Worth was concerned and asked us to follow up with you regarding your flight with us on March 11. We can understand how frustrating this trip must have been. Simply, we are very sorry for the inconvenience as a result of the delayed departure of flight 1808.*
>
> *As a frequent traveler, you know that good customer service sets us apart from the other airlines. So, when we don't provide it, no excuse will do. Although we will never compromise safety for the sake of on-time performance, we sincerely apologize that your travel plans were disrupted while traveling to Washington, D.C.*

We don't want to lose your confidence in us and hope you won't let this trip do so. Therefore, as an indication of how important your patronage is to us, I have added 7,000 Customer Service Bonus miles to your AADVANTAGE account. You should see this adjustment on one of your next two summaries.

Please continue to travel with us often. It is always a privilege to welcome you aboard.

Sincerely,

William R. Hodges
Executive Office
American Airlines

WOW! Four things earned the level of Win-Back Impression, **big time,** about this letter:

1. First, the airline actually monitored my flight and knew that I had experienced a mind-boggling delay. Sure, they knew the entire airport was shut down, but this was personal. They acknowledged *my* inconvenience.

2. Secondly, the airline apologized for an initial event that was completely out of their initial control.

3. Next, they asked me to continue to be their customer. The letter ends with: "*Please continue to travel with us often.*"

4. And finally, to ensure my loyalty, they *gave* me something—7,000 miles. And that's something to talk about. Seven thousand

> miles is one-third of the miles required to earn a round-trip frequent flyer ticket!

Do you think American won back this temporarily disgruntled customer with a letter like that? Oh yeah! In fact, I fly American almost exclusively now, rarely even rate shopping for competitive airline service.

Strategy: *Identify Customers On The Brink Of Defection And Go and Get Them!*

What American Airlines did so successfully is identified a customer on the brink of defection and launched a campaign to keep me—*one customer*—from leaving.

After American successfully won me back, I began to research the airline's win back strategy, as I knew their wooing wasn't random or accidental. It didn't take me long to discover that American has a smart strategy creatively named *WinBAAck,* where a system constantly monitors customers, searching for a decline in flight activity or to spot problems customers have experienced with their flights. The WinBAAck team personally contacts customers whose business has dropped off or those who have experienced unusual problems. I'd say the program is a tremendous success.

Don't let unhappy customers walk away without trying to determine why they're leaving, because they're taking vital revenue with them.

American's win back program is pointed, immediate and multi-faceted. Most companies, however, just let unhappy customers walk right out the door.

Case in point: Four months ago I walked into a branch of my bank, of which I'd been a customer for more than 15 years, and closed out my business checking account. My request was honored immediately and the deposit counselor laced the transaction with, "*It's a beautiful day*" and "*Have a great weekend,*" pleasantries. Within 15 minutes, I was officially a defected customer walking out the door, wondering why no attempt was made to keep my business.

As an absolute "customer loyalty advocate" and leadership development advocate, I naturally analyze and study customer service encounters in everyday transactions in pursuit for better ways businesses can relate to and retain their customer base. In this situation, my analysis highlighted three points:

- ✍ *The bank employee didn't even ask why I was leaving.*

- ✍ *There was no attempt to save the account.*

- ✍ *The employee, with her very friendly attitude, gave me the impression that she was actually eager to close out my account. (i.e., eager to say goodbye to me and my money.)*

The lack of response to my departure by this bank is a regrettable scenario that is played over and over again every hour in businesses around the world. Customers leave and companies make no attempt to find out why the customer left, and they certainly don't try to win them back.

What most companies don't realize is they are putting a significant amount of revenue at risk by letting customers leave without trying to save them.

A recent study by Marketing Metrics has shown that companies have a much better chance of winning business from their lost customers than from new prospects. On average, companies have a 20% to 40% chance of selling to lost customers, and only a 5% to 20% probability of selling to new prospects.

A recent participant of my *Loyalty Advantage* seminar knows talking to lost customers can result in PROFITS.

> *"Last year we lost a huge restaurant account. We had a good relationship with the customer, and they were satisfied with our work. However, a new regional manager came in and made the call to switch vendors. While the employees we dealt with weren't happy with the switch, they had to follow the new boss' lead. We have always made it a practice to visit and dine in our client's restaurants, and when the contract with this client ended, I worked to maintain the relationship. I would drop by for lunch or dinner, occasionally. While there, I'd visit with the manager and staff and even asked how things were going with the new vendor. I also invited the client to call on us should they ever need our services in the future. Well, it turned out the new vendor provided nothing but dissatisfaction to the restaurant, and when their contract ended with this company, who do you think the regional manager called? You got it! We won the customer back, and I know that is because we sustained the*

> *relationship and kept communicating with the customer, even after they left us."*

I later discovered that the actions taken by this employee to win this profitable customer back were actually unscripted, and he had no objective other than to maintain goodwill with a former client. Although one may not have thought there was a strategy, this very natural customer relations skill is a foundational strategy that can be called ***customer relationship management***.

Customer relationship management involves building loyal relationships with customers, continually working to strengthen the bonds of loyalty, maintaining loyalty after a service mishap, and should the relationship end, aggressively seeking to reunite with customers.

When customers defect, find out why they've left. By analyzing lost customers, you can develop an at-risk profile and then develop a focused customer relationship strategy to market to those customers.

For example, in *Customer Winback*, authors Jill Griffin and Michael W. Lowenstein discuss customer turnover at a large bank. The bank found that a significant proportion of its lost customers were the affluent, older and long-term customers. When these customers defected, they took all of their accounts and services with them. When the bank identified the profile of the defecting customer, it quickly launched a retention effort that targeted customers who fit the profile and hadn't yet left the bank and that helped protect against further defection of this profitable base of customers.

Develop and launch a customer win back strategy to identify and regain the goodwill of lost customers and you will watch your customer base and profits grow exponentially.

If your business has a records system (file cabinet, bankers boxes with files, electronic customer retention records management system, etc.) of lost accounts, inactive accounts, then consider any one of these immediate six engagement tactics for use in your marketing, sales, customer service and Service-Leadership© programs for blending into your activities work to incorporate potential new business. Use the following **BLENDS model:**

1. **B** = The best time to reach out to dialogue with a lost account is immediately after a winning engagement with a key account. That added **BOOST** in energy will be conveyed in your enthusiasm and may serve as a magnet to draw the past account back into a level of interest with you now.

2. **L** = Send a **LETTER** to each inactive account reintroducing yourself to them and two explosive new products or services you offer since they last interacted with your business. Then use these as the basis of additional customer contact work in the following days; this is a great tie in with Rule 1/12/50© (see Chapter twenty-two).

3. **E** = Review the evidence in their account records to determine exactly what precipitated their departure from our business. From this **EVIDENCE** you may see possible re-engagement opportunities to win them back.

4. **N** = Position yourself as a value added resource to each lost account and offer to provide a **NEEDS ANALYSIS** from your unique industry

perspectives to possible ways to increase their operational productivity or profitability by considering the use of some of your products or services

5. **D** = Just **DO** something for that business that will be seen as a value-added gesture as a way of earning back their attention, time and possible patronage.

6. **S** = Provide them with a **SAMPLE** of what you do as a way to entice them back and a means of gaining even a small piece of business with them once again.

The real value in the Win-Back is learning what the real value is to an organization in terms of bottom line dollars and cents. Recognizing the financial amount associated with a lost customer can become shocking, and this may become a compelling motivator for the "Service-Leader" to work diligently to keep a customer.

It's Just One Lost Customer. What's the Big Deal?

An example: Imagine you bring in a cleaning service to clean your home.

When they depart you find mildew still in the shower, smudges on the floor, dust throughout the house and a strange residue on your counter tops. Your first thought may be: *"I paid for this! Heck, I could have done this myself!"* Then you reflect upon your intentions when you called the company a week prior of signing up on a weekly plan for $240 per month. However, when you called back to complain as the upset or ballistic customer, the manager was polite, slightly apologetic, but did not guarantee your satisfaction, and when you told him you'd certainly not move forward with the plan for weekly service, he said absolutely nothing. This actually happened to Myra.

Here's what *they* just threw away:

1. One lost customer at $240/mo; $2880/year.

2. I will tell 11* people about my dissatisfaction.

3. My 11 friends will tell 5* people each.

4. My influence reaches 66 people (11 plus 55).

5. About a quarter (17) of the people I influence will never do business with *them.*

6. Here's how much the company will lose from me and 17 other people (who also abhor housecleaning) who would likely spend $240 a month: <u>$51,840.</u>

**TARP, Inc. found that unhappy customers tell an average of eleven people about their dissatisfaction and that those eleven people tell five others.*

This final dollar amount is a means to determining the "Value of a Customer" or what some may qualify as the "Lifetime Value of a Customer," as well.

To determine your customer value and the necessity of Win-Back strategies run the following formula on your client base:

1. Identify a typical customer (by name) you serve? ____________________

2. Determine a typical transaction with that customer, in terms of dollars associated with that transaction? $____________________

3. Identify the normal number of times that transaction takes place each month? ______________

4. Now, multiply the above numerical factors in question number two (2 x 3). $______________

5. Now, determine how many years that customer has been with your organization? ______________

6. Now multiply the numerical factor in question five times the number in question four. $____________

This final financial number becomes your benchmark as a "Service-Leader" in giving you and those around a better perspective and appreciation of your customer connections. This is for your organization an example of the "Lifetime Value of a Customer" to you.

Do you get the idea? One lost customer really is a *big* deal!

In business, it's not how many customers you win, it is how many customers you keep!

The average company in the U.S. loses half of its customers every five years (Frederick Richheld, The Loyalty Effect, 1996). Considering it costs four to six times more to acquire a new customer than to retain or win back an old one—and given the significantly higher probability of successfully selling again to lost customers than to prospects—it only makes sense to develop a customer win back plan.

Here are **Six Easy Steps to Win Back Customers** :

1. **Track customers who leave.** The first step of a win back program is to know exactly which customers are leaving and how many. Tracking defection is not just counting the lost, but it's what those numbers are telling you. It's about identifying the defected customer's buying patterns, tenure and net worth to the company. This tracking prepares you for step two.

2. **Develop an at-risk profile.** Analyze lost customers and look for common denominators, patterns and trends among the defected group. For example, the bank in our earlier example found that more than 20% of its lost customers were over 55, had been with the bank for more than ten years and had held multiple accounts. This valuable information must then be disseminated to the group responsible for customer retention so loyalty marketing efforts can focus on communicating with current customers who match the profile of high defectors. Those (at-risk) customers can then be protected from defection.

3. **Identify early warning signs of defection.** In many industries, customers on the brink of defection can be detected by one or more factors. For example, a banking customer who has stopped her automatic drafts and direct deposits and whose average monthly balance drops significantly might be tying up loose ends and heading to a competitor. Discover what factors suggest *your* customers are on their way out, so you can proactively communicate with them and entice them to stay.

American Airline's WinBAAck intelligence told them that frequent flyers that experience serious delays might be on the brink of defection. Therefore, the company quickly initiated communication with me and offered a goodwill token (7,000 bonus miles) to entice me to stay.

NOW, I ALWAYS FLY AMERICAN AIRLINES!

4. **Choose win back candidates.** Determine which defected (or on the brink of defection) customers the company wants to win back. Not all defected customers will be a love loss. There are some customers you're not positioned to create superior value for, and let's be honest, some customers you just don't want back. By selectively choosing win back targets, you can focus and maximize your efforts by going after only your best-fit customers.

5. **Go get 'em!** Develop and hold regular customer win back campaigns in order to win back customers, and learn why customers are leaving. Put together a team to personally call your best customers who have left and survey. (*What's prompted you to leave us? Where are you going? What attracts you to___?)* Next, invite the customers to come back. Overcome objections they give you and assure them that you can and will deliver the level of service they expect and deserve.

6. **Follow-up with all win back candidates.** When you win customers back, follow-up 30, 60, and 90 days after reuniting to ensure you are delivering the level of service they expect—service that will keep them for life. For the customers you don't win back, follow-up with a hand-written note thanking them for their past business and for the information they provided you after leaving.

Don't just let customers leave. Get proactive, set up processes to analyze lost customers and look for common denominators, patterns and trends among the defected group. Then, strategically use this new information for loyalty marketing efforts that will focus on communicating with current customers who match the profile of high defectors so those (at-risk) customers can be protected from defection.

When "Service Leaders" combine acquisition efforts with a strong win-back program, they can create a competitive advantage based on the strength of their service strategy.

Chapter Twenty-One

"Moments of Truth" and One Percent Factors to Ensure "Service-Leadership©" Mindsets and Behaviors

This chapter is about cultivating a "Service-Leadership" mindset and proactive behavior by all customer contact professionals through "Moments of Truth" understanding.

Simply put, "any exposure a customer has to you" is a moment in time captured in their mind as a "Moment of Truth." It can be positive or negative. Either way, it is a moment captured in time. It defines you in that customer's mind.

To ensure that the moments projected to your Vital Few and useful many customers are as positive as possible, take inventory of what the routine behaviors are in the course of your engagements and whether they are positive or negative.

What moment impressions are projected into your head as the recipient of someone who:

1. Approaches someone in a professional setting with the shirt disheveled, hair distractingly messed up, and has body odor?

2. When you bring a concern to a supposed customer service provider, and they immediately retort with the old, "… that is not my responsibility?"

3. Sees another person from a distance not offering to assist someone in obvious need of assistance, when they appear to be fully capable of assisting?

4. Encounters a professional establishment and the entry area is littered with obvious trash and dirt?

5. Calls a major business and the phone rings endlessly with no response/answer?

6. Sits politely at a restaurant, observing the wait staff engaging customers all about you while never coming to you?

Each of these is powerful impressions upon you both mentally and physically, and leaves a lasting "Moment of Truth" upon you. What is also critical to recognize is that each only took a matter of seconds to convey, yet yield a possible lifetime impression upon you.

A "Moment of Truth" then is any experience, action and response that a customer has from us. To ensure success loyalty, allies and success in competitive markets it is incumbent upon the "Service-Leader" to strive to make each and every moment a positive high stock value experience. While a moment is the event and impression, it is a series of behaviors that lead to the final moment.

Simple One-Percent Factors are the behaviors that with a mere one percent effort administered in a constructive manner, can ensure that the moment comes across in the most positive light possible.

For every moment that radiates outward from you, reflect on both the present one percent that cause you to attain positive "Moment of Truth" stature and all of the one percent behaviors if adopted that can increase your impact.

Revisit the above list of Moments and craft a list of One-Percent Behaviors that could have converted each simply from a negative and into a positive.

To enhance the Service-Leadership effectiveness of present customer service stars and enable others to aspire to the level of greatness that lies within them, consider how "Moments of Truth" apply to an organization's four core missions statements or MAPs (as detailed in Chapter Two) and when engaging the constituencies within each:

1. ***Organizational***—The core stakeholders to an organization that have vested financial interest and serve as the senior leadership team are charged with crafting this mission statement.

2. Functional Business Unit—Each work area to an organization should also have their own mission statement, which fosters, supports and contributes in its own unique manner to "organizational" mission statement or purpose.

Everyone within that business unit contributes to this one knowingly or not. And, thus, their actions are moments captured by those around them, and subsequently, influence other's actions.

3. Customer—This can be a moving fluid target for many service providers, so the key here is to be able to recognize independent of previous engagements, when you are face-to-face with a customer, "What is their purpose, need, want, mission statement and how do I fulfill that?" And, thus, what are your moments and one percent factors that can lead to an effective "Service-Leader" engagement?

4. Colleague—To recognize the core motivational reasons why the colleague you interact with is employed, reveals to you how to engage them to encourage their participation in providing W.O.W.® levels to customers.

It is this engagement and subsequent actions that are seen as moments by others.

"Moments of Truth" and the accompanying One-Percent Factors make or break an organization.

Chapter Twenty-Two

Fifty Plus W.O.W.®
Ways to Grow Your Business Now

Winning customers for life demands a continuous approach to connecting with customers on multiple levels, and a readiness for recognizing that at any time a customer service growth opportunity may present itself. As a "Service-Leader" being ready to communicate or create an atmosphere conducive for customer service exchanges to occur is your new norm.

As a "Service-Leader," tactically everything you do is a "Moment of Truth" in the customers' minds-eye and is a business growth opportunity.

Here is a rolling business growth action sequence. As you review it, check-off those that you are presently doing. Notice as you check them off, whether your competition does so. If so, you are at par. When you are done with a cursory review, notice those that are not checked off (indicating presently being deployed by your organization), and ask yourself how best to administrate that action plan (consider this a One Percent Factor). More importantly, as a USF, ask yourself if your known competition or even a new competitor to your market is actively and presently using that tactic?

***… W.O.W.®** any act that rises to the level of,*
***"Wonderfully Obvious What's"** …*
those "what factors" that compel others to want an
experience or item from you!

Here are **Fifty Plus Business Growth W.O.W.®** tactics for increased market share that you can deploy now:

1. **Rule 1-12-50©** - The first portion of every month (hence the number 1), consistently every month (hence the number 12), identify a population index upwards of fifty (hence the number 50) key customers or emerging customers and provide them a value added communication.

2. **eSignature Line** – Consider adding into your standard email auto signature line any updates on products or services you provide to all recipients of your communication exchanges. This also serves as a powerful standardization for ensuring customers receive advance notices for deadlines, product or service announcements, changes and discontinuations, etc.

3. **eAuto Responder** - Consider adding into your standard email auto responder (if you don't engage it routinely, especially engage it when you will be away from email receiving) any updates on products or services you provide to all recipients of your communication exchanges. This is also a great way to promote and advertise to those people that initiate sending email traffic to you first, as now you can instantly bounce back a message to them.

4. **Business Card Marketing** – Every time you correspond with a raving fan, send them three business cards with a note that one is for their records and to please forward the other two to someone they know that they would recommend to you.

5. **Hotel Letters** – Realize that in most all hotels there seems to be at least pieces of stationary and envelopes in the desk drawer. Consider a hand

written note to three "Vital Fews" about something that is top of mind to you and of value to them.

6. **"Advocate" Maintenance** Ensure that you never let an advocate get more than 30 days out from hearing from or seeing you. Plan regular communications and/or "thank you" events to draw from them ways to continue to enhance the service you provide to them.

7. **Direct Mail and eDirect Mail Marketing** – On a regular basis look for low cost and high impact ways to keep your name top of mind with your customer base and do so in innovative ways. Whether it is simple direct mail cards, newsletters, flyers, letters, reference and endorsement letters, etc.

8. **eZine** – Design a high impact, value rich content based electronic newsletter for your core customers (the Vital Few) and send weekly to them as a premium service and way to enrich their value proposition in their market. Then, soft communicate a product/service from you to them at the end of each electronic newsletter.

9. **Newsletter** – Design a high impact, value rich content based print newsletter for your core customers (the Vital Few) and send routinely to them as a way to enrich their value proposition in their market. Then, soft communicate a product/service from you to them at the end of each newsletter. This vehicle can be distributed to customers as statement-stuffers, attachments with invoices and contracts, attached to proposals and general correspondence from customer service contact professionals and the sales team alike. This

can serve as a source for the Rule 1-12-50© campaign.

10. **Connect** – Look deep into your network of advocates and recognize from your vantage point whether you have customers that can actually interact with one another and benefit one another. By you connecting them together, it raises your stock value in both of their eyes, and thus, may create greater business opportunities for you.

11. **Fax Alerts** – Consider a Friday afternoon fax blast to your customers with any products/services that can impact their bottom line, send announcements and press releases, etc. If these contact names are in your data base as clients and or contacts that you have a pre existing relationship with and/or have established a relationship with whereby they want communication offers from you, than a Fax alert or blast is a smart, fast, economical and acceptable contact means. Conversely, if you don't have this rapport or permission then a fax blast may be seen as spam and be illegal in some non business growth oriented communities!

12. **Website Exposure** – Make sure you have an electronic way for electronic commerce to take place 24/7 and make sure it is designed to the needs of 'your' "Vital Few." Don't take advice from anyone else in the universe nor design an exposure that is all things to all people. Success leaves clues, and successful electronic commerce sites will yell what works and what does not work.

13. **Affiliate Connections** – Cultivate as many affiliate relationships with businesses with similar clients as yours and with whom the networking connection

can yield business growth opportunities for both you and your affiliate. The affiliate connection should be one where the mutual relationship raises each other's stock value in the market.

14. **Upgrade Your "Vital Few"** – Continuously evaluate ways to enlarge market share from your core customers and attract your competitor's core customers by recognizing that many times there are high impact gestures you can extend to customers that are actually low level 'give-away' items, upgrades, premiums, etc. from you. An upgrade to a first class seat to a most frequent of frequent flyers to an airline is a negligible cost, yet yields significant psychological (emotion investment, see Chapter One) dividends with the customer.

15. **Certificate Investment** – Consider appropriate investments into your customer base at multiple levels that entices customers from the "Useful Many" to the "Vital Few" to want to come back for your USF© offerings; upgrade options, discount for volume purchases, discounts or special pricing or add-ons for long term partnerships, premium offerings to affiliate partners, services for special relationships with you, etc. These short-term acts yield long-term gains and are loyalty-building gestures that may, in many cases, be the seeds from which your "advocates" come from in the future.

16. **Content Press Releases** – Always keep your five mission statements clear in mind for your industry trade publications and community press. When opportunities for you to take the lead as subject matter experts and service/product providers rise to be quoted in the press or deliver helpful editorial content makes itself available, seize that exposure.

For print press, always make sure that your contact name, phone, fax, email and website address are easily distinguishable from the text.

17. **Walking Billboard** – Consider, as appropriate, as often as possible to have your contact name, logo, eAddresses visible on clothing, luggage, business cases, and any other non-traditional places for your footprint.

18. **Frequent Customer Program** – Consider ways to recognize and reward your "Vital Few" and entice your "Useful Many" to ascend into "Vital Few" volume customer status. The sole purpose of this program is to entice future business, cultivate loyal legions of customers and create an energy force around being a customer partner with you, that new customers begin migration patterns away from your competition and toward you.

19. **Sale** – Everyone likes a sale, especially if they feel they are getting a great deal. So, in anticipation of rate or fee increases, make sure you communicate to your most valued customers – "Vital Few" – an opportunity to make additional purchases or commitments under the old fee.

20. **Gift Time** – Some organizations have policies that preclude customer service providers from extending a sincere "thank you" act towards their customers, in part, due to the decades of scrupulous individuals on both sides of the transaction. When appropriate, look for meaningful exchanges of a tangible item that will be remembered long after the exchange dissipates. Those items that bring real value to the customers' professional life are most impactful.

21. **Vital Few Referral** – At every opportunity of completely fulfilling a need put to you from this demographic, requests for referrals from their network could likewise benefit from your offer. Then immediately use that as the source of your customer contact follow up.

22. **Service Beyond the Sale** – If your service and communication with customers stops with the sale, you are also stopping future business opportunities with customers. Provide customers with follow-up service. Make care calls, thank customers for their business, and follow-up to see how you might *continue* to be of service.

23. **Create Value** – Customers today want more than a transaction, they want a good return on their investment when they do business with you. Make sure customers see the value of your products and service delivery. If there is no real value, what sets you apart from your competition?

24. **W.O.W.® Customers** – Strive to not only meet customers' expectations, but also work hard to exceed them. Carl Sewell, owner of the legendary Sewell Cadillac dealership in Dallas, is known for W.O.W.®ing customers and turning one-time buyers into customers for life. How does he WOW customers? Technicians are on call 24/7 to respond to customers in need. He has 150 loaner cars so customers are never without transportation, and he even has a restaurant on site to occupy customers' time should they choose to wait for their vehicle.

25. **Statement Stuffers** – Always include in any correspondence to customers, billing account

invoicing, Request For Proposals/RFP, past-due notices, etc., a simple enclosure that announces your newest service or product offering. Rotate this initiative every month, so that it is automatic and always current.

26. **Bounce Back Direct Mail Cards** – Always include a postal direct mail card (replicate this same process with an electronic direct email promotional vehicle) with anything you send out that allows for an interested party to solicit more information from you on what you do or offer.

27. **Bonus Bounce Back Direct Mail Card** – While following the same purpose as above, here you would be directed by a comment on the card or adjacent to the card in your ad layout in a newsletter, article, letter, etc., to provide the request for more information style bounce back card to a "friend" or "colleague" that the recipient perceives as possibly gaining value from your offer.

28. **Pass Along Coupons** – Create a coupon that your best customers would receive that they could in turn give to their best customers to gain from your services at a special discount or pre-market availability date. Design it in such a way that they could even write their name on the coupon as they give it to the recipient.

29. **Affiliate Partnership** – Immediately identify a non-competing business that could benefit from your customers and likewise, whom you could benefit from connecting with their customers. Then forge a partnership whereby you can reciprocate exposure either by deploying any one of the above

techniques or other collaborative marketing contact activities. And do so today.

30. **Theme Event Tie In** As pubs do with theme tie-ins to St. Patrick's Day or Cinco de Mayo, and retail stores do with any holiday, look for an appropriate calendar holiday, industry highlighted date or community celebrated region date, and build a marketing awareness and celebration event around that date and event to draw additional attention to what you offer, thereby raising awareness in the consumers minds and additional transaction traffic to your place of business.

31. **Exit Interview** - Send an exit interview questionnaire to any lost customer, immediately, via email, direct mail, telephone follow-up to determine reasons for leaving you as a vendor.

32. **Monthly Win-Back (earn back their business) Coupons** - Offer each month a coupon or offer to any customer that leaves you to regain their business or a portion of their business back.

33. **Create an Award** – Consider creating an awareness community achievement award for someone who exemplifies great "?" and present it periodically. Then, send out press announcements, etc., thereby raising the public's awareness and attention to who you are.

34. **Partnerships** – Consider a partnership with a local radio station, television station, community/suburban newspaper or major daily newspaper in your community for business unique specials.

35. **Chamber of Commerce Membership Accountability** – Regularly review any business association membership, such as your city's Chamber Of Commerce, and determine if you can make a "direct identification" to business gained as an affiliation with that group or business maintained. If not, then actively communicate to them as to what services and programs they have to raise your awareness in the minds of their other members and prospects in that community, as well as by residual efforts, those that are not members. If the case can not be aggressively made that there are immediate business growth vehicles available by that Chamber, "step out" of your membership immediately as that Chamber is only interested in them selves, and you are throwing away your money. Take your otherwise budgeted money and test joining a suburban chamber of commerce rather than your own community or don't do either and use that money in another business growth campaign as detailed previously among this list.

36. **Friends and Family First** – Design a special network of key advocate customers that you test all specials, coupons, and functions with before going live with your larger audience. This will allow you to fine tune any offering or endeavor and will create word-of-mouth buzz about your initiative before the big launch.

37. **Trade eMail Blasts** – Evaluate who you know on a personal and professional level that may have a data base of contacts that could be served well by your product/service and offer to develop a weekly or monthly marketing special that they would send on your behalf as a special announcement to drive

interested parties to you. Conversely, you would do the same for them.

38. **Sponsorship** – Consider sponsoring a group, sporting team, individual that your name, logo and contact information (email address, website address, phone number and/or address) being made visible by them would place your name in front of suspects and prospects to what you offer. In making your determination, consider sponsorships and your name placement where there is the greatest ongoing exposure with the greatest residual pay off to you.

39. **Signage** – Consider how you position yourself based upon signage for public consumption and get strategic and innovative. For example, if you had a place of business or a competitor on one side of you display a large sign stating, "World's Largest Inventory" and the vendor on the other side of you posted signage, "World's Lowest Prices Everyday," then you would be smart to make an even larger sign that reads, "Enter Here!!!"

    Consider the color and placement for maximum impact. Fast food restaurants have learned that reds, yellows and oranges stimulant hunger and they all pattern their signage accordingly. Casinos know flashing lights attract, and more importantly, they post their signs in a way that it can be seen from every traffic pattern and from a distance

40. **Software Systems** - Engage business growth research and networking software systems that may otherwise be out of your financial reach. For example most local libraries have explosive software systems for market research, trends analysis, contact information that costs tens-of-

thousands of dollars to subscribe into that you can access and many times free!

41. **Mass Merchandise Promotions** – Consider innovative and inexpensive point of purchase brand awareness and influence instruments within your business. For example if your in a restaurant, then table tents promoting specials, new high profit items (dessert, drinks) that are available should be promoted.

42. **Public Access Signage** – Consider simple yet compelling window posters (even a simple 8x10 sheet of paper posted is better than nothing!) of up coming events, product and service introductions, specials. Co-promote with other businesses, retailers, merchants in your niche or neighborhood to cross promote to their customers and further drive customer service traffic among your community.

43. **Pool Promotion Money** – Work with your business neighbors that are in your same geography (retail mal or strip center collaborations), same industry, or supply chain sequence of businesses that all interact to move a final service or product to create a pool of financial assets to enable one to purchase radio, television, print, direct marketing, etc.

44. **Special Invitation** – Consider opportunities for the product or service that you provide and cross analyze the Vital Few customers that you have and make a personal phone call, send an email or drop by and see them with a personal invitation, coupon, certificate, discount offer to draw them back to you for a repeat business opportunity.

45. **Media Celebrity Status** – Explore your uniqueness that would be of interest to your community or industry and develop an on going list of contacts that you can avail yourself to for powerful quotes, interviews or even a regular series within their medium on business growth strategies, in exchange for your business contact information being made available for their audience to connect with you.

46. **Media Partnerships** – Building upon "Media Celebrity Status" consider the newspapers, magazine, journals and electronic newsletters that your customer base is exposed to and begin penning powerfully unique articles that immediate impact your audiences financial bottom line and routinely write and offer them for publication. Make sure your contact information always appears on each page of your article and request from the publishers that this data appear within or at the end of any articles they use.

47. **Inspire Word-of-Mouth Advertising** - Customers who experience Beyond WOW service will tell five people about their experience. If you fail to meet customer's expectations, eleven people will hear about the service breakdown. But if you drop the ball with a customer and **come back with a WOW recovery**, customers will tell seventeen people about the recovery...that's more than three times as many people they'd tell if the service was Beyond WOW initially. Resolving complaints can be one of your best ways to generate positive word of mouth advertising and we all know word of mouth advertising is "THE" most persuasive form of advertising.

48. **Ask For Complaints** - An interior design firm includes a post card with all product orders that reads *"Please complain. If your order was late or wrong or if any of goods were damaged in the slightest, please call our customer care hotline."*

    The owner of this firm knows that ninety-five percent of complaining customers will remain loyal if their problem is resolved immediately and to their satisfaction (as shown by research by TARP, Inc.) Further research has shown that complaining customers who have their problems resolved become more loyal to the company than if no problem had occurred at all. Making it easy for customers to complain and offering quick resolutions is an easy way to protect customers from defecting to the competition and increase loyalty.

49. **Follow-Up With Complainants** - The company's idea of problem resolution may not necessarily be the customer's idea of a satisfactory resolution. For this reason, it's a great idea to follow up with customers who complained 30 – 90 days after you've resolved the problem to ensure they are satisfied with your resolution. This extra step helps you capture problems that weren't identified at the initial point of contact and helps you completely regain customer goodwill after service mishaps.

50. **Give A Token Item** - Coupons and product samples have a definite impact on loyalty after a service failure has occurred. A study conducted for the Society of Consumer Affairs Professionals found that 58% of complaining consumers who received something in the mail following voicing their complaint to the company were delighted, versus only 40% of those who did

not receive anything. Giving customers token items, such as coupons or product samples, after a service failure both increases the perception of value and serves to maintain loyalty.

As detailed above, as a "Service-Leader" tactically everything you do is a "Moment Of Truth" in the customers' minds-eye and is a business growth opportunity in respect to immediate opportunities and long-term possibilities for your business and colleagues.

To further enhance the impact of these immediate business growth strategies and tactics, you should also consider:

1. Aggressive affiliation with any local and national trade associations appropriate to your business industry.

2. Aggressively associate with individuals you meet within these associations that have like minds with yours and with whom you can forge informal networking groups (similar in nature to a mastermind group as detailed in **POWER CHARGED FOR LIFE** by Dr. Jeffrey Magee) that you can workshop needs, concerns, and possible new product/service introductions to improve each initiative before actualization.

3. Actively reach out to your local municipality government and affiliated organizations that my have business growth development groups, agencies, retired business leader's that serve in an adjunct mentor consultation capacity and open yourself for their input!

4. Immediately make sales training a regular and consistent component of your daily business life.

> Provide regular year long sales training t everyone that comes into contact with your customers to enhance their present skill set and provide skills to those lacking formal training in this area (consider ***THE SALES TRAIING HANDBOOK: 52 Quick, Easy To Lead Mini-Seminars***, by Dr. Jeffrey Magee and published by McGraw-Hill. ISBN #0071375163 / US $99.95)

Always look for business growth opportunities, whether as an extension of something you do already to attain greater productivity and profitability or something completely new!

PART Seven: Understanding the Business of Business

Chapter Twenty-Three—
Building the Front-Side (Physical) and Back-Side (Emotional) of W.O.W.®

Chapter Twenty-Four—
Growing Your Business by Knowing Your Customer

Chapter Twenty-Three

Building the Front-Side (Physical) and Back-Side (Emotional) of W.O.W.®

Understanding the business of the customer service business has everything to do with understanding the overall operational business model of business. Your true beliefs of customers and customer service leaves a footprint on every aspect of business and at every level within a business if it truly is charged with delivering an ***"Exceptional"*** customer care rating! (see Chapter Six and the CSI model.)

To understand how every action, process, event and person leaves their footprint upon customer service, visualize a traditional business pyramid.

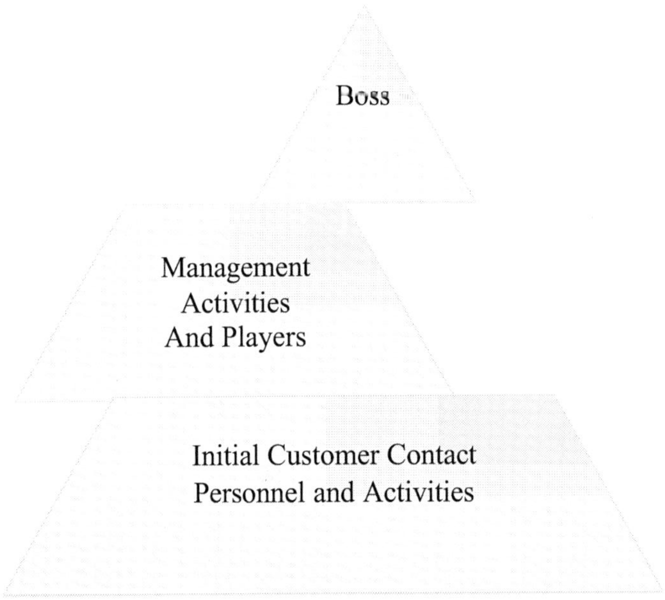

With this traditional business pyramid, the business of the business is very top down directed, and in many instances, the senior leadership (Boss) is so far removed from the actual functionality of that business' purpose, that they begin to loose their pulse of what brought them to the market. They also become very jaded in what makes the business reality, as players become intimidated by leadership and instead of having open healthy interactions, mid-level managers and frontline functionaries only communicate upward what they believe or perceive is what is wanted to be heard.

To get a better and more accurate picture, invert the pyramid and recognize that the people closest to knowing the customers' needs and frustrations are the very people in the old model at the bottom. It is the initial customer contact personnel. In the new model, these customer service contact professionals become the top of the inverted model and should be the first in line for skill tune-up opportunities, resource allocation and empowerment opportunities.

Visualize this inverted pyramid as a funnel. This funnel will serve as a Business Activity Funnel, and you can make three broad generalizations or categories about the funnel and then attribute everything about business into an appropriate category.

1 =

2 =

3 =

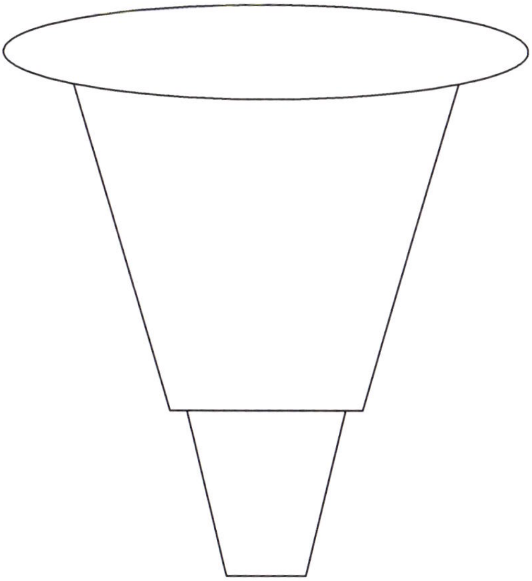

To enhance the level of customer service sought or mandated, look into each category and ask the relevant questions about Mission Statement, MAP, Win-Back, four ways to differentiate, application of the Reliable CARE© formula, and so forth, into each category.

Your "Business Activity Funnel" represents three categories and all of the associated types of customer activities and functions:

1. Level #1 of the funnel represents the entry point of customers, promotions, networking, advertising, marketing campaigns and programs being rolled-out, community service awareness activities, branding initiatives, etc. as it relates to either getting your name out into your target market or your market coming to you.

2. Level #2 of the funnel represents interactions with existing customers, selling, order processing, engaging of upset customers, follow up and follow through initiatives, up selling and cross selling activities, servicing accounts, etc.

3. Level #3 of the funnel represents all of the administration, account maintenance endeavors, behind the scenes meetings and endeavors that support the business and why the "Vital Few" come to you, survey management, accounts payable and accounts receivables, hospitality initiatives, etc.

Winning customers for life demands a continuous commitment toward professionalism as a "Service-Leader" in today's marketplace. It is paramount that everyone realize that every activity, no matter where it lie in the funnel, has its own associated "Moments Of Truths" and has a residual effect on subsequent endeavors.

Go forth and strive to go ***BEYOND W.O.W.® and build the essential "Service-Leadership©" approaches to exceptional customer service performance and lasting relationships***!

Chapter Twenty-Four
Growing Your Business, by Knowing Your Customer

Drawing upon the strategic and tactical ideas detailed herein, ***BEYOND W.O.W.***®, will allow a business the necessary tools to enhance an existing success factor and others a map to success if that is truly what is desired.

Growing your customer base starts with the application of these ideas to enable the *"Service-Leader"* within you to shine. The following game plan is suggested for truly understanding your customer and guiding your business growth actions to cultivate more like them.

Start by isolating from your customer base an ideal customer for this final exercise. An ideal (reference Vital Few) customer would be one that, if you could replicate getting more of them, it would be a 'grand-slam'!

Now, with that single specific customer in mind, take a blank sheet of paper (electronically, open a new word file and label it with the identified customer), and make a large inverted L-Grid across the top of that page. Now, across the top label it with the customer's name. Within the inside of that L-Grid, do a complete brain-dump of everything you know about them personally and/or professionally.

To motivate the volume of content about that ideal customer you have identified for this exercise, reflect upon the 5W and 1H model learned in grammar school.

Once you have exhausted that exercise with the individual line-after-line entries of "stuff" you have attributed to them, take that exercise sheet of "your answers" on "your customer," and now, on the outside left hand side of that page with the inverted L-grid data, to the left side of the page now create an appropriate "category" for that descriptor.

Once you have attributed each entry to an appropriate identity category, you have created an Ideal Customer Profile, based upon what is presently working for you. Now, with these descriptive "categories" listed, you can take this as a template and let that guide your future Q&A interactions with any perspective suspect, prospect or repeat customer. You have proven the minimum types of or category of information that you need to conversationally learn in order to forge effective and lasting customer relationships!

To fine-tune this PROFILE for growing your business through improved customer service, focus, and "Service-Leadership" effectiveness from every employee (frontline through to the top line), consider:

1. Develop your Profile.
2. Develop a departmental Profile.
3. Develop and organizational Profile.
4. Benchmark each off of one another for consistent "categories."
5. Survey actively, repeatedly, consistently and continually, until death do you part. This will allow you to ensure the integrity of what you do.
6. Identify for each client their Mission Statement. (Maintain this in your contact data base, client information management system, or merely keep it

top of mind.) Let this be a benchmark for how you engage them and why you engage them.

7. Know who your Profile customers' primary and secondary benefactors are and why they are coming to you. Benchmark all services you provide to them from this information.

8. Understand your Profile customers' annual growth or net earnings for this year, previous year(s) and benchmark that against their projections for this year.

9. Dedicate yourself to Rule 1-12-Profile: Meaning, make sure the first portion of the month (hence the number one), for every month (hence the number twelve), that you send some sort of personalized communication to all of your active Profile customers.

Maintaining W.O.W.® with your customers starts with knowing your customers. Getting BEYOND W.O.W.® requires knowing your customer is dependent upon the leader within you showing up to work. The critical differentiator in the business place today and tomorrow will most definitely be CUSTOMER SERVICE provided by a true Service-Leader!

For More Information on Scheduling Myra Golden or Jeffrey Magee for Your Needs, Contact:

Myra Golden works with organizations that are serious about increasing customer profitability. Her training programs position employees at all levels to build and maintain loyal relationships with customers, quickly regain customer goodwill after service mishaps, and even win back lost customers. Her clients include Arvest Bank, the FDIC, Proctor & Gamble, Scotts LawnService, and Vistakon, a division of Johnson & Johnson.

Myra is the former head of Customer Care for Thrifty Rent-A-Car System, Inc. where she led a strategic team of customer loyalty advocates who successfully regained the goodwill of unhappy customers and she worked with the company's loyalty program to create value for the most frequent customers. While at Thrifty, Travel Magazine named Myra a Rising Star.

She can be reached by email at Myra@MyraGolden.Com or by calling 866-873-8419.

For Additional Information:
MYRA GOLDEN SEMINARS
3729 S. 195th E. Ave.
Broken Arrow, OK 74014
Toll free 1-866-873-8419
www.myragolden.com

Dr. Jeffrey L. Magee, PDM, CSP, CMC, is a highly sought content rich platform speaker, author, consultant, and syndicated leadership columnist. Jeff works with individuals and businesses that wish to greatly increase their productivity and profitability through business and leadership training without limits.

He can be reached at either his personal email address Jeffrey@JeffreyMagee.com, or telephone toll free 1-877-90-MAGEE or visit his website at, www.JeffreyMagee.com .

His client's include the leading Fortune 500 firms (such as Pfizer, El Paso Energy, IBM, GMAC), major Associations (such as ABA, WESTERN CPE, FCCS, NYFEA), and the largest leadership development organizations in the World – the United States Junior Chamber and the United States ARMY.

The Department of Defense recently commissioned three of Jeff's leadership programs for training their senior officers, senior non-commissioned officers and an advanced recruiter selling course nationally to the United States ARMY National Guard's 5,000 plus recruiters.

For Additional Information:

JEFF MAGEE INTERNATIONAL/
***PERFORMANCE Magazine*/PERFORMANCE Publications**
P. O. Box 701918
Tulsa, OK, 74170-1918
Toll free 1-877-90-MAGEE
www.JeffreyMagee.com , and www.KeepingTheEdge.com , and www.WIIFM.us , and www.SquimToLearn.com

Resources

Look For These Other Resources

ADVANCING IN OUR CAREER: Developing Yourself, Designing a Winning Board of Directors & 25 Powerful Networking Steps For Success! By Jeffrey Magee, Performance Publications, ISBN #0-9641240-7-6/$15.95 – audio.

Building A Legendary Leader: 52 Steps To Crafting Managerial-Leadership Greatness, One Week At A Time! By Jeffrey Magee, Performance Publications, ISBN#0-9718010-2/$29.95 – book.

COACHING for IMPACT: Leadership And The Art Of Generational Coaching! By Jeffrey Magee & Jay Kent-Ferraro, Triumphant Publishing, ISBN#0-9641240-3-3/$29.95 – book.

ENOUGH ALREADY! 50 Fast Ways To Deal With, Manage And Eliminate NEGATIVITY At Work Or Home. By Jeffrey Magee, Performance Publications, ISBN#0-99641240-9-2/$12.95 – book.

How To Keep Customers Coming Back After Any Service Mishap. By Myra Golden, Maya-Salathiel Publishing/$59.95 – manual.

How To Keep Customers Coming Back After Any Service Mishap. By Myra Golden, Maya-Salathiel Publishing/$599.00 – trainer's kit.

Performance Driven Selling! By Jeffrey Magee, Performance Publications, ISBN#0-9641240-5-X/$49.95 – audio.

Power Charged For Life: Learn 10 Power Steps To Sustained Positive Mental Attitude. By Jeffrey Magee, Performance Publications, ISBN#0-9641240-4-1/$19.95 – audio.

Squirm to Learn: If You're Not Squirming, You're Not Learning! By David J. Simons, Jeffrey Magee and Ginny Simons, Performance Publications, ISBN#0-9718010-1-0/$12.95 – book.

The Sales Training Handbook: 52 Quick, Easy To Lead Mini-Seminars. By Jeffrey Magee, McGraw-Hill Publications, ISBN#0071375163/$99.00 – textbook.

What's In It For Me? Tuning Into WIIFM + Fifty-Two Powerful Ways for Young (ALL) Professionals to Advance in Their Career! By Jeffrey Magee & Damon Roberts, Performance Publications, ISBN#0-9718010-4-5/$12.95 – book.

YIELD MANAGEMENT: The Leadership Alternative for Performance and Net Profit Improvement. By Jeffrey Magee, CRC/St. Lucie Press, ISBN#1-57444-206-6/$39.95 – textbook.

Bibliography

Golden, Myra, *Customer Recovery: How to Keep Customers In Love After Any Service Mishap*, Myra Golden Seminars, Broken Arrow, OK, 2002.

Griffin, Jill and Lowenstein, Michael, *Customer Winback*, Josey-Bass, San Francisco, 2001.

Peters, Ed, *The 4Profit Speaking System*, 4 Profit Institute, St. Petersburg, FL, 2001.

Reichheld, Frederick F., *The Loyalty Effect: The Hidden Force Behind growth, profits & Lasting Value,* Harvard Business School Press Bain & Company, Boston MA, 1996.

Sanders, Tim, *Love Is the Killer App: How to Win Business and Influence Friends*, Crown Business, New York, 2002.

Technical Assistance Research Programs, Inc. (TARP), *Consumer Complaint-Handling in America: Final Report*, White House Office of Consumer Affairs, 1980.